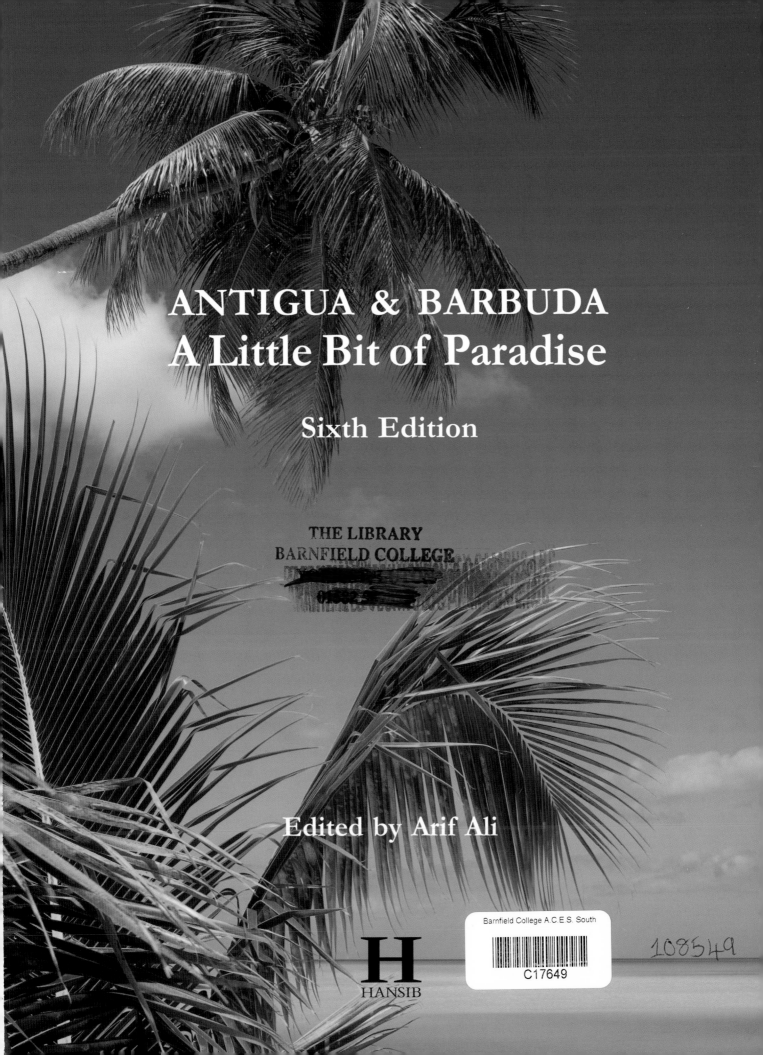

ANTIGUA & BARBUDA
A Little Bit of Paradise

Sixth Edition

Edited by Arif Ali

HANSIB

Published in Great Britain in 2008
London & Hertfordshire

Hansib Publications Limited
P.O. Box 226, Hertford SG14 3WY

Email: info@hansib-books.com   Website: www.hansib-books.com

ISBN: 978-1-906190-02-6

© Hansib Publications Ltd

Photographs © As individually credited

First edition published by Hansib Publications, 1988
Second edition published by Hansib Publications, 1994
Third edition published by Hansib Publications, 1996
Fourth edition published by Hansib Publications, 1999
Fifth edition published by Hansib Publications, 2005

Printed and bound in Great Britain

A welcome to the world

This publication brings new illumination to any image of Antigua and Barbuda, and indeed any concept of the Caribbean, you may already have. Antigua and Barbuda is more than a little bit of paradise.

Antigua and Barbuda is an ever evolving mosaic of a region that is widely recognised as a world of its own. Nowhere else in the Antilles will you find so concentrated a mix of the essences of the Caribbean archipelago.

Antigua and Barbuda is a cosmopolitan mecca that welcomes and is enriched by people and cultures from all over the region and the world; each endeavouring, all achieving, as our national anthem affirms. Visitors will find renewal and rebirth in twin tropical islands ringed with an extravagance of superb beaches and in the spirit of a people who are uniquely spontaneous and welcoming.

Having made a decisive break with its past in 2004, Antigua and Barbuda is redefining itself as a country committed to new standards of governance as we gear up for the opportunities offered by the Caribbean Single Market and Economy and the Free Trade Area of the Americas.

We welcome the world to an ongoing celebration of the quintessential Caribbean experience and to ready access to business opportunities well beyond the Caribbean.

This publication is an engaging and authentic rendering of Antigua and Barbuda at a new dawn in the new century.

I look forward to welcoming you, as visitor and investor, to this little bit of paradise and to our two islands of opportunity.

The Honourable Baldwin Spencer
Prime Minister of Antigua and Barbuda

Prime Minister Baldwin Spencer is pictured with the University of West Georgia marching band during Antigua and Barbuda's 25th anniversary of independence celebrations in 2006. The band was performing at the United States Air Force base located near V.C. Bird International Airport.

Photo: Photogenesis

A little bit of paradise . . . revisited

Harold Lovell
Minister of Tourism,
Aviation, Culture &
Environment

Welcome to the sixth edition of *Antigua and Barbuda: A Little Bit of Paradise*. This latest publication reflects the dynamism, change and renewal evident in Antigua and Barbuda today. Our mission is to enhance our national image to stimulate business opportunities and to create a balanced people-centred social environment.

A specific thrust of the Baldwin Spencer administration is the development of tourism in its various facets – the friendly and hospitable approach of our people will be harnessed in renewing our commitment to our guests, providing a quality visitor experience. This, coupled with the superior accommodation choices, excellent sailing opportunities and onshore cruise options, makes Antigua and Barbuda the ultimate destination.

The airport is our major gateway and we completed Phase 1 of the refurbishment and modernisation of this facility in April 2007. Phase 2 will include major work on the runway, parallel taxi-way and apron on the airside and, subsequently, the construction of a new, ultra-modern terminal building.

In 2007, we successfully hosted six Super-Eight matches as part of the Cricket World Cup Tournament and Antigua and Barbuda was also proud to be the sole venue of the Stanford 20/20 Cricket Tournament. Both events were beamed to audiences worldwide. The Antigua Sailing Week and the Classic Yacht Regatta continue to attract some of the world's largest and most technologically advanced yachts, and in December 2006 we hosted our first annual Super Yacht Cup Regatta. These events, together with the Annual Charter Yacht Meeting (The Boat Show), make Antigua and Barbuda the premier yachting destination in the Caribbean.

Our calendar of cultural festivals presents an interesting selection of our best artistic pursuits. These include our summer Carnival, Barbuda's Caribana, the Homecoming Festival, Moods of Pan Festival, Independence Cricket Fest, Christian Valley MangoFest and the Antigua and Barbuda Literary Arts Festival.

We are inviting investors to participate in the growth of the economy and have provided a climate for easy navigation with the establishment of the Antigua and Barbuda Investment Authority. We are especially pleased to encourage our nationals living in the diaspora to make a significant contribution to the building of a new Antigua and Barbuda.

We expect that *A Little Bit of Paradise* will be situated in a prominent place in every Antiguan and Barbudan household, here and abroad, so that we as citizens can continue to appreciate this wonderful piece of heaven we call home.

A Little Bit of Paradise will be a valuable resource for every person with an interest in this country and will ignite a love and passion for its beauty through the portrayals of serene island life with a global perspective.

You will enjoy this journey through our diverse landscape, history and culture.

RIGHT
Minister Harold Lovell poses with US television personality Oprah Winfrey during one of her many visits to Antigua and Barbuda.

FACING PAGE
The beach at Valley Bay has all the characteristics of Paradise on Earth.
Photo: Joseph Jones

Acknowledgements

I am grateful to the following for their help and support with the production of this 6th edition of *Antigua and Barbuda: A Little Bit of Paradise*:

Firstly, I should like to thank **Prime Minister Baldwin Spencer** and the **Antigua and Barbuda Cabinet** for commissioning this new edition of *A Little Bit of Paradise*. Special thanks are also due to Minister of Tourism Harold Lovell, Permanent Secretary Sharon Zane Peters and their staff for their support throughout the preparation of the book.

Thanks are due to **Managing Editor Kash Ali** and Co-ordinator Isha Persaud.

To Richard Painter of Print Resources, Shareef Ali of Graphic Resolutions, Moti Persaud and Ian Marsh.

To our main photographer Joseph Jones; to Susan Matthias, Colin Cumberbatch, Bobby Reis, Ella Barnes, Fidel Persaud, Franklin Benjamin and his staff at Heritage Hotel; to E.M. Grimes-Graeme, Barbara A. Arrindell, Alan Cross, Cecil Wade and his staff at Amaryllis Hotel, Chandani Persaud, Joe Antonio, Lucy Marsh, Nandani Persaud and to Pamela Mary for caring so much.

To our contributing writers (in alphabetical order): Barbara Arrindell, Sereno Benjamin, Mickel Brann, Veneta Burton, Sir James Carlisle, Rachel H. Collis, Rasona Davis, Kim Derrick, Ivor Ford, Franklin Francis, Bruce Goodwin, Roddy Grimes-Graeme, Edward T. Henry, Joanne C. Hillhouse, D. Giselle Isaac, D. Annette Michael, Dr Reg Murphy, Dorbrene O'Marde, Dr Ermina Osoba, Kevin Silston.

To our contributing photographers (in alphabetical order): Antigua and Barbuda Tourism Department, Brooks La Touche Photography, Mark Day, Yvonne Fisher, Eli Fuller, Ann Granger, Roddy Grimes-Graeme, Janet Jones, Joseph Jones, K. Maguire, Joseph Martin / Photogenesis, Maurice Merchant, Reg Murphy, Matteo Torres / Stanford International Bank, Snapshots Imaging / M. Henery, David Vrancken, Martha Watkins-Gilkes.

Arif Ali

FACING PAGE
A picturesque residence in the southern village of Liberta.
Photo: Joseph Jones

Supporters

Hansib Publications is grateful to the following individuals, businesses and organisations for their support with this 6th edition of *Antigua and Barbuda: A Little Bit of Paradise*

Abbott's Jewellery
18 Heritage Quay, St John's
Tel: 462 3107 Fax: 462 3109
Email: abbottsoffice@candw.ag

Amaryllis Hotel
Sir George Walter Highway
Tel: 462 8690 Fax: 462 8691
Email: amahotel@candw.ag

ABI Financial Group
156 Redcliffe Street
P.O. Box 1679, St John's
Tel: 480 2700/85 Fax: 480 2746
Email: abib@abifinancial.com

Antigua Computer Technology Co Ltd
TeleDome Building
Old Parham Road, P.O. Box 3090
St John's
Tel: 480 5228 Fax: 480 5232
Email: sdoumith@actol.net

Antigua Hotel & Tourist Association
P.O. Box 454, Island House
Newgate Street, St John's
Tel: 462 0374 Fax: 462 3702
Email: neil@antiguahotels.org

The Best of Books
Lower St Mary's Street, P.O. Box 433
St John's
Tel: 562 3198 Fax: 562 3198
Email: bestofbooks@yahoo.com

CCCS Ltd
Casada Gardens
P.O. Box 1247, St John's
Tel: 725 0251
Email: cccsmoti@gmail.com

Colombian Emeralds
Heritage Quay, St John's
Tel: 462 7903 Fax: 462 3351
Email: ematthews@dutyfree.com

Department of Marine Services & Merchant Shipping
P.O. Box 1394
Corner of Popeshead & Dickenson Bay Streets, St John's
Tel: 462 1273 Fax: 462 4358
Email: marineserv@candw.ag

Global Bank of Commerce Ltd
4 Woods Centre, P.O. Box W1803,
St John's
Tel: 480 2207/480 2240 Fax: 462 1831
Email: bsy@gbc.ag

Governor General's Office
Government House
Independence Drive, St John's
Tel: 462 0003 Fax: 462 2566

Hadeed Motors Ltd
Old Parham Road, St John's
Tel: 481 2526 Fax: 481 2519
Email: admin@hadeedmotors.com

Heritage Hotel
Heritage Quay, St John's
Tel: 462 2262/1247 Fax: 462 1179
Email: heritage@candw.ag

Madison's Casino
Runaway Bay
St John's
Tel: 562 7874 Fax: 562 4574
Email: doylecarter@gmail.com

The Map Shop
St Mary's Street, St John's
Tel: 462 3993 Fax: 462 3995
Email: cesmap@candw.ag

Ortho Medical Associates
Woods Centre, St John's
Tel: 460 7720/462 1932
Fax: 461 8065
Email: ortho@candw.ag

Quin Farara & Co Ltd
P.O. Box 215, St John's
Tel: 462 3198 Fax: 462 2704
Email: quinfarara@candw.ag

Stanford International Bank Ltd
11 Pavilion Drive, St John's
Tel: 480 3783 Fax: 480 3726
Email: mkhouly@stanfordeagle.com

Taino's Art Gallery & Gift Shop
Jolly Harbour Shopping Centre
Jolly Harbour
Tel: 562 5851

Town House Furnishings
Market Street, P.O. Box 2730, St John's
Tel: 462 1560/562 4932 Fax: 462 5239
Email: Edward.townhouse@gmail.com

**Wadadli Enterprises Ltd/
Kennedys Club Ltd**
Casada Gardens, c/o P.O. Box 364,
St John's
Tel: 481 1300 Fax: 481 1325
Email: neil.cochrane@kennedysclub.com

West Indies Oil Company
Friars Hill Road, St John's
Tel: 462 0440 Fax: 462 0543
Email: wiocjf@candw.ag

International dialling code for Antigua and Barbuda: 268

Contents

Map Key

Main Road	
Secondary Road	
Other Road	
Track	
Runway	
✈	Airport
⚓	Customs & Immigration
• Police Stn	Police Station
⛽	Gas Station
Ⓑ	Bus Station
PO	Post Office
Sch	School
✝	Church
Ⓗ	Hospital
🚦	Traffic Light
△▽	Trigonomical Station
★	Point of Interest
⚓	Jetty/Jetties
	Beaches

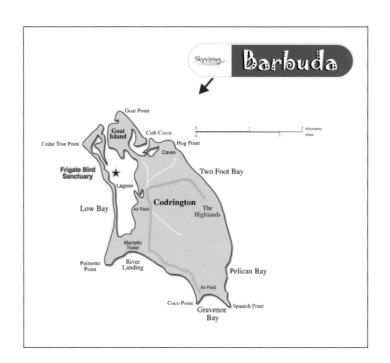

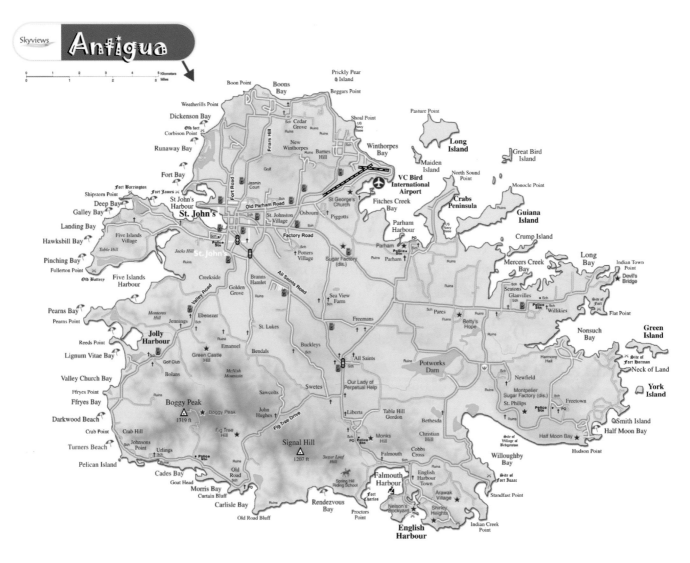

Foreword

The three hundred and sixty five beaches in Antigua and Barbuda are just the beginning. Add the people's hospitality, smiles and laughter; add quality accommodation at all levels; add the internationally acclaimed cuisine; add the efficient facilities for business. All are there to see and feel from the moment you arrive at the refurbished V.C. Bird International Airport, under the watchful eye of the four National Heroes; or when you arrive by sea at Heritage Quay amid the hustle and bustle of St John's where traditions stand side-by-side with modernity.

The Ministry of Tourism and environment are putting plans into place to upgrade facilities at the former sugar plantation Betty's Hope, and to develop Devil's Bridge as quality attractions. Improving the facilities at various beaches continues with immediate plans for seven beaches – Friars, Fort James, Long Bay, Morris Bay, Jabber Wok, Pigeon Point and Darkwood.

You can hear nationals and visitors commenting on the new look of the capital with its fancy pavements and street signs, and the traffic congestion, with the hope that completion of the new car park will help ease the problem.

The improvement in St John's seems to be infectious; spreading beyond the city to the villages and inspiring the Prime Minister Baldwin Spencer to say, privately, that he will consider re-introducing the 'Best Village Competition', which was very popular some years ago. As you travel around the country you will see a new pride to keep Antigua and Barbuda tidy.

The 2007 Cricket World Cup may have encouraged some of what is happening, but the government and people have grasped the opportunity with both hands and gone further.

The 20/20 Cricket World Cup, which was held in South Africa in September 2007, was a great event. However, Antigua and Barbuda can claim a first in this field: one of the country's nationals, Sir Allen Stanford, organised the world's first international 20/20 cricket competition in Antigua in 2006 with over a dozen countries taking part. Guyana was the first winner, receiving US$ 1 million as first prize. Sir Allen's competition has put back some needed inspiration and funding into West Indies cricket which will benefit the area for years to come. The second Stanford 20/20 Cricket Tournament will be held in Antigua in early 2008.

In 2007, the country celebrated the 50th anniversary of Carnival in Antigua and Barbuda. The festival is now described as one of the great street festivals in the Caribbean. The nation also celebrated the 40th anniversary of Antigua Sailing Week, now one of the world's top five sailing regattas. The country also celebrated the 40th anniversary of the Police Service.

An event that I found of great interest earlier this year was when Prime Minister, on an overseas visit, appointed Dr Jacqui Quinn-Leandro to act as Prime Minister. Dr Quinn-Leandro was sworn in by the newly-appointed Governor-General Her Excellency Louise Lake-Tack. On that occasion the Governor-General, the Acting Prime Minister, the Chief of Police, eighty percent of the Permanent Secretaries, the Ombudsman, the Director of Audit, the government's Senior Analyst, the Chief Protocol Officer and several others in government and the private sector, were all women. This must have been a world first and one which other nations must surely follow.

It is worth noting that this twin-island state, with its population of 75,000, attracts over 700,000 visitors each year; in other words, the country plays host to ten times its population. Little wonder, then, that several hundreds more hotel rooms are becoming available and dozens of real estate projects are underway.

This pictorial reflection of Antigua and Barbuda is an insight into the beautiful beaches, fantastic sunsets, warm evenings and moonlit nights; the lingering cool breezes that will leave you with memories of a little bit of paradise.

Arif Ali
Heritage Hotel, St John's, Antigua
September 2007

Facts and Figures

Full Name
Antigua and Barbuda

Area
442 sq km (170 sq miles) [Antigua 281 sq km;
Barbuda 161 sq km]

Location
The twin-island state of Antigua and Barbuda
is situated between the Caribbean Sea and the
Atlantic Ocean in the Leeward Islands chain.
Antigua is the largest of the Leeward Islands.
Barbuda is located 30 miles north of Antigua.

Population
69,481 (July 2007 est.)

Capital
St John's

Nationality
Antiguan(s), Barbudan(s)

Language
English

Religion(s)
Anglican 25.7%, Seventh Day Adventist 12.3%,
Pentecostal 10.6%, Moravian 10.5%, Roman
Catholic 10.4%, Methodist 7.9%, Baptist
4.9%, Church of God 4.5%, other Christian
5.4%, other 2%, none or unspecified 5.8%

Ethnic Groups
African heritage 91%, mixed 4.4%, white
1.7%, other 2.9%

Literacy
85.8%

Currency
East Caribbean Dollar (EC$ / XCD)

GDP per capita
US$ 10,920 (World Bank, 2006)

Government
A constitutional, Westminster-style
parliamentary democracy. The bicameral
legislature comprises a 17-member House of
Representatives elected every five years and a
Senate of appointed members. The United
Progressive Party (UPP) won elections held
on 23 March 2004 by a majority of 12 seats to
4 with one seat (Barbuda) tied. There was a
return to the ballots in Barbuda where the
Barbuda People's Movement subsequently won
and now supports the UPP government.

Main Political Parties
United Progressive Party (UPP), Antigua
Labour Party (ALP), Barbuda People's
Movement (BPM)

Head of State
Her Majesty Queen Elizabeth II represented
by HE the Governor-General, Louise Lake-
Tack.

Prime Minister
The Hon. (Winston) Baldwin Spencer

Foreign Minister
The Hon. (Winston) Baldwin Spencer

Administrative Divisions
Six Parishes: Saint George, Saint John, Saint
Mary, Saint Paul, Saint Peter, Saint Philip

Public Holidays
New Year's Day
Good Friday
Easter Monday
Labour Day (May)
Whit Monday
Carnival Monday (1st Monday in August)
Carnival Tuesday (1st Tuesday in August)
Independence Day (1 November)
Heroes' Day
Christmas Day
Boxing Day

Events

Antigua Yacht Club Round the Island Race (Jan)
Black History Month (February)
Antigua Open Golf Tournament (March)
Antigua Classic Yacht Regatta (April)
Antigua Sailing Week (April / May)
Caribana, Barbuda (May)
Antigua and Barbuda Sports Fishing
Tournament (May)
Calypso Spektakula (June)
Carnival (July / August)
Wadadli Day (July)
Royal Antigua and Barbuda Police Force Week
of Activities (September)
Annual World Gospel Festival (October)
National Warri Festival (October)
Independence Day Parade & Food Fare (Nov)
V.C. Bird Day (December)

Important Dates

Independence from Great Britain –
1 November 1981
Joined the Commonwealth – 1981

Membership of international organisations

ACP, CariCom, CDB, Commonwealth,
ECLAC, FAO, G77, IBRD, ICAO, ICFTU,
ICRM, IFAD, IFC, IFRCS, ILO, IMG, IMO,
Intelsat (non-signatory user), Interpol, IOC,
ITU, NAM (observer), OAS, OECS,
OPANAL, UN, UNCTAD, UNESCO, UPU,
WCL, WFTU, WHO, WMO, WTO. Antigua
will assume Chairmanship of the G77 in 2008.

Major Industries

Tourism, construction, light manufacturing,
offshore financial services

Main exports

Agricultural, light manufacturing, fisheries, rum

Major Trading Partners

Export: Caricom countries, European Union
Import: Caricom countries, European Union,
United States, Canada, Central & South
America, Asia

Media

Press: Antigua Sun, The Daily Observer
Radio: ABS Radio, Observer Radio, Caribbean
Radio Lighthouse, ZDK Liberty Radio, Sun
FM, Crusader Radio, Vybz FM, Latin FM,
Hits FM, Nice FM, Radio Paradise
Television: ABS-TV, CTV (cable), Karibe Cable

National Flower

Agave blossom (aka: Dagger Log or Batta Log)

National Bird

Magnificent frigate bird (aka: man-o-war or
weather bird)

National Animal

Fallow deer

National Sea Creature

Hawksbill turtle

National Fruit

Antigua 'black' pineapple

National Dish

Pepperpot and fungee

National Motto

"Each endeavouring, all achieving"

Climate

Tropical, with little variation between the
seasons and broadly defined as 'wet' or 'dry'
seasons. The twin-island state lies within the
hurricane belt

Time Zone

GMT -4 hours

Highest Point

Boggy Peak (402m)

Internet Country Code

.ag

International Dialling Code

+1 268

National symbols

NATIONAL COAT OF ARMS

The Pineapple on top of the heraldic helmet represents the famous Antigua black pineapple. The Red Hibiscus flowers are symbolic of the many varieties of this plant found in abundance on the islands. The Shield with the Golden Sun and wavy blue and white bands of the National Flag symbolise the sun, sea and beaches for which Antigua and Barbuda are renowned. The Old Sugar Mill and the stem of sugar cane have historical roots and depict the cultivation of sugar cane for the production of sugar, which was Antigua's main industry. The Yucca plant or 'Spanish bayonet', with its upright stem and showy edible flower cluster at its summit was the old emblem of Antigua. The deer are symbolic of the wildlife that inhabited pre-colonial Antigua and Barbuda. The scroll bears the motto of the nation, "Each endeavouring, all achieving".

DESIGNER OF THE COAT OF ARMS

The National Coat of Arms was designed by Gordon Christopher with a little modification by the Statehood Celebrations Committee, 1966. Mr Christopher was born in Antigua and emigrated to Canada in 1967.

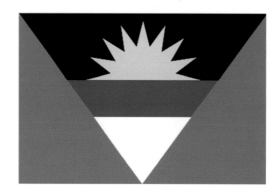

MOTTO OF THE NATION

The motto of the nation is, "Each endeavouring, all achieving". It was composed by James H Carrott MBE in 1967 when he was Permanent Secretary in the Ministry of Trade, Production and Labour. According to Mr Carrott, "The concept was to provide inspiration to each Antiguan and Barbudan to recognise that the development of the whole country would be a benefit to all, but that development required the effort of each individual."

NATIONAL FLAG

The golden sun image symbolises the dawn of a new era; red symbolises the dynamism of the people; blue represents hope; black symbolises the soil and the nation's African heritage; gold, blue and white represent Antigua's natural tourist attractions - sun, sea and sand; and the 'v' shape symbolises 'victory'.

DESIGNER OF THE FLAG

The flag of Antigua and Barbuda was designed in 1967 when the country became a State in Association with Britain. Its designer, Reginald Samuel, is an Antiguan artist, sculptor, painter and art teacher. His design was selected from among 600 entries.

National anthem

Words by Novelle H Richards,
music by Walter P Chambers,
arrangement by H A Kenney.

Welcome to Antigua and Barbuda

D. GISELE ISAAC

Of Antigua and Barbuda's small, interconnected society it used to be said, "If you go back far enough, *everybody*'s related." And today, the relatives have returned for a grand reunion, where the faces from the Dominican Republic mix with those whose origins are in Africa, Europe and the Middle East.

Way back when, searching for economic opportunity, our grandfathers and their brothers journeyed to Santo Domingo to cut sugarcane. Many were never heard from again, until their offspring came home to claim their birthright. And so, in the primary school classrooms, Davis sits ahead of Diaz, and Pena and Peters are best friends.

At Saturday market, Antiguan women buy vegetables from Dominican vendors; walk up-town to shop in Lebanese and Syrian stores; then flock to Spanish salons for their Sunday morning hairdo, before picking up a takeaway dinner of Chinese chicken chop suey or Jamaican jerk pork.

Light years ahead of the integration movement, this 170-square mile, twin-island nation is, without fanfare, a multi-national, multi-ethnic, multi-racial community.

Numbered among the new immigrants – the Spanish, Chinese, Africans, Guyanese and Jamaicans – are hundreds of Americans and Europeans, who now outnumber the native-born descendants of Portuguese and Scottish merchants. Some came, like Columbus, on voyages of discovery, but decided to drop anchor – often in the picturesque seafaring communities of English Harbour, Falmouth Harbour and Cobbs Cross in the south-east and, increasingly, Jolly Harbour in the south-west.

The burgeoning population has spread out across the island, creating communities where canefields and cow pastures once stood. The abandoned windmills – all that remains of the defunct sugar estates – are testament to the decline of agriculture and the rise of other, less labour-intensive industries, like banking, insurance, telecommunications and aviation, which have helped to build a solid middle-class.

In 1983, Antigua and Barbuda took the lead in the Eastern Caribbean in establishing diplomatic relations with the People's Republic of China. The two countries have since enjoyed very friendly relations, offering support to each

RIGHT
Not just for motorists, the sign on the road to Darkwood Beach could apply to all who visit Antigua and Barbuda.

FACING PAGE
St John's Cathedral dominates the capital's skyline. Built in the mid-1840s, it came into service in 1847 and was consecrated in 1848.

Photos: Joseph Jones

Located on Barbuda's west coast, Palm Beach stretches for fourteen miles.

Photo: Joseph Jones

other in the international arena. Over the years, China has provided assistance which has funded many construction projects including the Exhibition and Cultural Centre, YASCO Sports Centre and, more recently, the Sir Vivian Richards Cricket Stadium in time for the 2007 Cricket World Cup. It is expected that the good relations between the two countries, based on equality and mutual benefit, will continue to grow and will bring more tangible benefits to the peoples of both countries.

Tourism, however, remains Antigua and Barbuda's main industry. Cooled by tropical breezes, the sun-drenched islands are home to some of the world's most spectacular beaches – 365 white-sand treasures on Antigua and pristine, pink-sand getaways on Barbuda.

The sister-island also boasts an environmentally sound lagoon that is home to a well-preserved sanctuary for frigate birds and a population of fallow deer.

With an international airport that services most of the major carriers, travel into and out of Antigua and Barbuda is easy and direct. And for the commercial traveller, advanced telecommunications such as broadband Internet and direct-dial international telephone, and conference facilities, make doing business almost a holiday.

Cruise-ship passengers, meanwhile, make the most of their stopovers by shopping in the capital's duty-free port; dining at the many excellent restaurants; exploring historic sites like the ruins at Fort Shirley and Nelson's

Dockyard, a restored Georgian museum and boat yard; horseback riding; swimming with stingrays in the Atlantic; or kayaking around the northeast coastline.

As locals have become more affluent, leisure activities have increased and diversified. However, certain pastimes remain almost sacred. Antiguans and Barbudans abroad plan their visits home in July and August to coincide with Carnival, billed as "the Caribbean's greatest summer festival," and, over eleven days, Antigua revels in a celebration of colourful masquerade, energising steelband music, sweet and/or satirical calypso anthems, and cathartic street dances that sweep away differences of race, creed and class.

For Barbuda's similarly structured carnival, Caribana, held earlier in the year, Antiguans decamp to the sister-island for a weekend flavoured with choice lobster, crab, conch, and venison.

Air arrivals are probably greatest in April, when Test cricket and Sailing Week generally take place. Cricket at the history-making Antigua Recreation Ground (ARG) is, itself, a festival where winning and losing are merely incidental to the day-long parties at which libation, food,

laughter and music flow. The ARG will now be used for other national activities. International cricket moves to the new Sir Vivian Richards Cricket Stadium which was built in time for the Cricket World Cup in 2007.

Meanwhile, Antigua Sailing Week – one of the world's top five regattas – attracts 'yachties' and boating enthusiasts from across the globe, transforming English, Falmouth and Jolly Harbours into hives of fevered activity. The spring Boat Show, during which the world's most luxurious vessels are on exhibition in Falmouth Harbour, is quite an experience for those buying and those looking on in wonder.

"Homecoming," the country's latest festival, was introduced at Independence 2004. The celebration centred on community pride, national institutions and icons, and significant historical events. As well, it featured entertainment that included zonal beauty pageants, a GospelFest, and a gala banquet and dance. Based on its success, it is expected to become an annual event.

Antiguans and Barbudans are traditionally Christian, and no matter how late into the morning the Saturday night party runs, church attendance on Sunday is generally robust. While

TOP
The first port of call for cruise ship passengers is Heritage Quay and its excellent duty free shopping.

FACING PAGE
Jolly Harbour is an impressive development which includes an 18-hole championship golf course, full service marina, shopping centre, restaurants and bars, villas and a wide range of sports facilities.
Photos: Joseph Jones

Antigua and Barbuda's capital, St John's, was the first city in the British West Indies to be laid out in the grid system. Since its establishment it has developed into a world class financial hub as well as an attractive and popular duty free shopping centre.

Photo: Joseph Jones

the Anglican Cathedral of St John's dominates the city, the Methodist, Moravian, Catholic, Adventist, Baptist, Wesleyan, Lutheran and Pentecostal churches peacefully co-exist with smaller congregations like the Baha'i, Muslims and Hindus.

Apart from being the keepers of souls, the churches also play a part in keeping the culture. The Anglican and Moravian Food Fairs, for instance, are national events at which the culinary arts are equal parts exhibition and consumption. It is here that the immigrant communities come into their own, offering treats as varied as Japanese sushi, Dominican mountain chicken, Montserratian kiddie stew, and sarsaparilla, an aphrodisiac, from the Kittitians. And, of course, local favourites like souse and rice (blood) pudding; fungie and shad; and doucana and saltfish have a very short shelf life.

These events are not just church fund-raisers; they are very real self-affirmations, reassurances that, despite the encroachment of North American values, cable television and the Internet, we are still West Indians where it counts – at stomach, at heart, and in spirit.

PREVIOUS PAGE
Viewed from Shirley Heights, English Harbour is one of the best and safest natural anchorages in the Caribbean. It has been used since the late 1600s and, today, is a hive of activity – especially during Antigua Sailing Week.

THIS PAGE
Participating vessels at their moorings during the Antigua Classic Yacht Regatta, top, and Antigua Sailing Week, right.

FACING PAGE
An idyllic sunset at the end of another day's sailing.

Photos: Joseph Jones

The majestic palm
trees of Morris Bay.

Photo: Joseph Jones

The roots of a vibrant culture

DORBRENE O'MARDE

Antiguans and Barbudans practise and exhibit a culture that reflects attributes from their African ancestry and heritage, the historical effects of British colonialism and the recent North American economic and political influences in the Caribbean region. The national culture is further informed by the physical factors of extremely small geographic size, relatively flat topography and tropical climate The synthesis of these influences – historical, biological, physical and psychological – has also yielded an emerging philosophy and cultural expressions that are, without doubt, uniquely Caribbean.

The range of cultural activities and experiences available in Antigua and Barbuda has broadened in the last twenty years through the influx of Caribbean peoples from other islands, notably Jamaica, Guyana, Dominica, the Dominican Republic and Montserrat. In addition, there has been growth in the Lebanese, Syrian, Asian, North American and European segments of the population but these migrants are more active in the economic life of the country than its popular culture.

The nature of the dominant cultural traits and those performing and visuals arts which depict the national culture, is African. The official language of the country is English but most Antiguans speak an English dialect that is sprinkled with African linguistic retentions and speech patterns. The steelband and calypso rhythms find roots in the centrality of the drum to African music and culture, and popular dance is made distinct by the preference for motion in the waist and the hips of dancers.

Antigua has witnessed, like many other Caribbean countries, a phenomenal rise in the popularity and political power of the new Christian 'religious right' that continues to challenge the traditional dominance of the established churches. Popular religious thought, however, still acknowledges the active existence of a spirit world and in Antigua there are remnants of the practice of *obeah*, an African based system of spiritual beliefs.

Traditionally, the Christmas period was the highlight of cultural creativity and production in the country. However, the Antigua Carnival,

RIGHT
Independence Youth Rally during the country's 25th anniversary of independence celebrations in 2006.

FACING PAGE
A shaded hang-out on the banks of Codrington Lagoon in Barbuda.
Photos: Joseph Jones

CLOCKWISE FROM TOP LEFT

Antigua and Barbuda
celebrated its 25th
anniversary of independence
in 2006. That year, the
annual independence
celebrations were treated
with added reverence.
Photos: Joseph Jones

LEFT
Prime Minister Baldwin
Spencer is pictured during
his official visit to Cuba in
2005 with students from
Antigua and Barbuda
studying in that country.

TOP
Today's fishermen still use
traditional fishing methods.

ABOVE
Independence Youth Rally.

RIGHT
Dominoes at the
West Bus Station.

Photos: Joseph Jones

staged annually during the summer period (July/ August) has, since its inception in 1957, replaced the Christmas period and associated festivities as the cultural focus. It is at that time of year and in a joint celebration of emancipation from slavery and summer tourism that Antiguans are at their creative best. It is at Carnival when composers create new music; when new dances evolve; when the graphic artists and costume and clothes designers blossom; when dramatic skills are revealed in both youth and adult pantomime and song presentation.

Antiguan musicians, in shared endeavour with other regional artists - mainly in the soca, calypso and steelband music forms, have made notable international impact in the furtherance of Caribbean culture. Soca group, the Burning Flames are presently the most popular and internationally recognised of Antigua musicians. The role of the calypso as a medium for both entertainment and socio-political development is heralded through national competitions that make national heroes of consistent winners. Sir McLean Emmanuel ("Short Shirt") was

TOP
The beautiful surroundings
of the Dockyard Museum
in Nelson's Dockyard.
Photo: Joseph Jones

ABOVE
With its roots in west Africa,
warri is Antigua and Barbuda's
national board game.
Photo: Joseph Martin

LEFT
The Museum of
Antigua and Barbuda.
Photo: Joseph Jones

TOP
Built in 1674, Betty's Hope is
the site of one of the first
sugar plantations in Antigua.
Photo: Joseph Jones

ABOVE
Roast corn vendor in St John's.
Photo: Photogenesis

RIGHT
Coates Cottage, which is
now an art gallery, was once a
barracoon (a type of barracks)
for the confinement of slaves.
Photo: Joseph Jones

knighted by the Antiguan government for mastery of the calypso artform. Other artists such as Paul Richards ("Obstinate") and Rupert Philo ("Swallow") have been given national awards for their calypso exploits also. Reggae and dance hall music are also important local and regional forms. Steelbands such as Hells Gate, Harmonites and Gemonites continue the tradition that heralds Antiguan bands as among the finest in the region.

There is a long tradition of drama in the Antigua society developed around the natural inclination of the population towards story-telling, recitation and the *'Singing Meeting'* where practitioners of verbal arts battle each other or laud their linguistic mastery over awed and appreciative audiences. However, there has been a decline over the last two decades of the practice of theatre arts. Creative writing is predominantly expressed through poetry and fiction and new writers, grappling with the establishment of a literary tradition and sensibility, are emerging. There is a minor tradition of the publication of social and political study and the practice of

TOP
The Mas Troupes gather during Carnival 2007.

LEFT
Live steelband entertainment at Shirley Heights.

Photos: Joseph Jones

journalism now struggles to find legitimacy in the newly found democratic environment.

The dance is once again popular. A number of dance groups such as the Antigua Modern Dance Academy, Shiva and the VS Dancers, inspired by regional and international influences and the 'dance of the street', regularly produce shows of exciting choreographed material.

Antigua, no longer a major producer of agricultural products, imports food from virtually every continent in the world. It offers a cuisine that is comparable to the finest regional and international fare. In addition, culinary artists, especially in the tourism sector, are interestingly beginning to recognise and utilise the foods and cooking methods of the native population in their creations.

Antiguans and Barbudans continue to battle the new and efficient forms of cultural penetration such as cable television and the US publishing industry with their values and value-systems that promote both social and economic dependence on products and thoughts generated externally. There is recognition in the country, however, that it is cultural uniqueness which defines and protects its national identity and confers viability on its participation in world affairs.

The 50th anniversary of Carnival in Antigua and Barbuda was celebrated in 2007. From its humble beginnings in 1957, the event has grown into one of the Caribbean's leading festivals.

TOP
Halcyon Steel Orchestra.

ABOVE
Calypsonian "Mighty Solo".

LEFT
Mahico Stars Steel Orchestra.

Photos: Joseph Jones

TOP
Carnival participants from
the Rastafarian community.

ABOVE
Calypsonian "Lord Franco".

RIGHT
Tanzania "Tizzy" Sebastian
entertains the crowds during
the Party Monarch competition.

Photos: Joseph Jones

St John's Cathedral
dominates the capital's
skyline during the day
and the night.
Photo: Joseph Jones

TOP
The distinctive, pink stucco-decorated, Catholic church of Our Lady of Perpetual Help in Tyrell's.

LEFT
The interior of St John's Cathedral is encased in wood in order to protect it from hurricanes and earthquakes. It served its purpose during the earthquake of 1974.

TOP
The bell of St Barnabas Church, in Liberta, was rung, most significantly, to celebrate the freedom of the slaves on Emancipation Day on 1st August 1834.

RIGHT
Sunday morning walk to church in Grays Farm.

Photos: Joseph Jones

47

TOP
A relaxing afternoon
at Ffryes Bay.

LEFT
Model yacht racing at
Falmouth Harbour.

Photos: Joseph Jones

48

Faces of Antigua.

Photos: Joseph Jones

TOP
League cricket at Mack Pond fields in All Saints.

LEFT
"Gravy" is a modern-day Antiguan icon whose enthusiasm for cricket is at the forefront of the game's support.

FACING PAGE
Soft ball cricket at Grays Farm.

Photos: Joseph Jones

Sunset cricket on
Fort James Beach.
Photo: Joseph Jones

Fifty years of Carnival

BARBARA ARRINDELL

Carnival in Antigua and Barbuda celebrated its 50th anniversary in 2007. This momentous landmark was acknowledged throughout the nation with added fervour and high spirits.

Back in the 1950s, the country was going through a period of significant change; the sugar industry was giving way to tourism as the leading driver of the economy, and the birth of carnival was on the horizon. In 1957, the first carnival took place and signalled the arrival of an event that would capture the hearts and minds of the people of Antigua and Barbuda for generations.

Under the leadership of John Shoul, one of Antigua's most successful businessmen, a team was pulled together to explore the idea of further developing the one-off carnival which was held in 1953 to commemorate the coronation of Queen Elizabeth II.

Dame Yvonne Maginley fondly remembers being asked to sit on the first carnival planning committee, a decision which she says altered the course of her life. In that first year, she accepted responsibility for what was called Children's Carnival. The following year she chaired both the Children's Carnival Committee and the Queen Show Committee. Other members of the committee organised a talent show, a calypso show, the parades, and J'ouvert ensuring that local bands, particularly the steelbands, had ample opportunity to be seen.

Another well known contributor to carnival was Keva Margetson, who states simply that carnival is in her blood; and if not in the blood, it was in the genes. History records that not only her parents and her siblings as major players, but her daughter, Patrice, sings with a leading jam band. For more than fifteen years, Keva's father (cultural icon Bobby Margetson) and his wife Rose, like others at the time, transformed their home into a mas camp every summer. On Carnival days the 'J'ouvert Revellers' would join the crowds 'jumping up' to the sounds of the Hell's Gate Steel Band, Brute Force, Harmonites, Halcyon, Superstars and Gemonites.

As one year made way for another, costume designers like Connie and Heather Doram, and costume creators from mas camps like Ali and

RIGHT
A fitting tribute to the 50th anniversary of Carnival in Antigua and Barbuda.

FACING PAGE
Solid International playing their 2007 Carnival theme 'Historia'.

Photos: Joseph Jones

Associates and Dynamics, found that they were
not only competing with other troupes, but they
were competing with themselves, trying to better
their creative genius of previous years. The
competition extended to every aspect of the
summer festivity.

Calypsonians pulled their supporters from
their respective villages and went to verbal war
with each other year after year. The longest noted
calypso feud took place in the 1970s when

"Short Shirt" and "Swallow" dominated the
stage, leaving many talented singers to fight for
third place. In more recent times, as ladies
entered and quickly rose to dominance in the
calypso arena, a similar contest evolved between
the four times crowned "Queen Ivena" and her
rival "Singing Althea".

The Lions' Den – the quiet home of one of
the island's most well established service
organisations – has for over twenty years been

CLOCKWISE FROM TOP LEFT

Trinidad's 'Carib Girls' attend Carnival each year to play with Extreme International Mas Troupe.

As a member of the Revellers Mas Troupe, Prime Minister Baldwin Spencer embodies the spirit of Carnival during its momentous 50th anniversary year.

Queen of Carnival 2007, Tasheka Lavann, with the 1957 Carnival Queen, Gloria Whyte-Margetson.

Tourism Minister Harold Lovell, right, among the throng of Carnival revellers.

FACING PAGE
Resplendent in her costume, 'The Prestige of Victory', Tasheka Lavann was crowned Queen of Carnival 2007.

Photos: Joseph Jones

transformed into the home of Antigua's most well known jam band, The Burning Flames. Here, thousands of party-goers assemble each night to dance under the stars until the break of dawn.

But through it all, as competitors clash on the stage and on the road, the coming together of people of all races, creeds and nationalities often provides the nation with a short reprieve from other more stressful activities.

Carnival in Antigua and Barbuda culminates on the first Monday in August, a public holiday set aside to observe Emancipation Day. The day and the celebrations are a constant reminder of the freedom gained by former slaves in 1834.

The festival attracts tourists from far and wide who find themselves dancing to the early hours or just sitting on the side of the road sipping coconut water with total strangers as the magic of Carnival casts its spell.

The contest for Queen of
Carnival is an explosion of
colour and pageantry.
Photo: Joseph Jones

TOP
The Parade of Mas Troupes
in Carnival City.

RIGHT
Blue Devils J'ouvert troupe.

FACING PAGE
A 'sinister' alternative to the
vibrant colours of Carnival.

Photos: Joseph Jones

Followers of the Blue Devils
J'ouvert troupe pack the
streets of the capital.
Photo: Joseph Jones

CLOCKWISE FROM TOP

Followers of the Blue Devils J'ouvert troupe.

Dynamics Mas Troupe with their theme 'Tribute'.

The Parade of Carnival Troupes and Groups.

FACING PAGE
Revellers Mas Troupe take to the stage.

Photos: Joseph Jones

TOP
Mahico Stars Steel
Orchestra.

MIDDLE
Passion Mas Troupe.

LEFT
Solid International playing
their theme 'Historia'.

FAR LEFT
Dynamics Mas Troupe.

Photos: Joseph Jones

TOP
Revellers Mas Troupe.

RIGHT
Former Queen of Carnival
Angella Degannes enjoying
Carnival 2007.

FAR RIGHT
Children's Carnival.

Photos: Joseph Jones

TOP
The stilt-walkers of Vitus
Mas Troupe, from the
Catholic Church, with
'The Midas Touch'.

LEFT
A Blue Devil reveller.

FAR LEFT
The Parade of Carnival
Troupes and Groups.

Photos: Joseph Jones

TOP
Extreme International Mas Troupe play their theme 'Rare and Extremely Brilliant'.

RIGHT
Mud Mas.

Photos: Joseph Jones

A wealth of musical talent

DORBRENE O'MARDE

The early forms of music in Antigua and Barbuda reflected the influences of African and European traditions. African song and dance traditions were brought to Antigua and the rest of the Caribbean through the slave trade and would play a major role in the development of Caribbean music styles.

The blending of these cultural forms resulted in the creation of 'bennah'. This style of music shares common characteristics with all other types of African-Caribbean music. Its form was that of the litany or call-and-response and its themes were dominated by praise, blame or ridicule. The songs tended to be improvised, and musical accompaniment was by drum or other percussive instrument.

The most famous of all bennah singers was John "Quarkoo" Thomas. During the 1940s and 1950s he sang the 'topic-of-the-day', which often echoed the feelings of the masses who were labouring under colonial rule. In traditional African fashion he used song to ridicule the oppressors and wrong-doers.

Bennah eventually came under the influence of the more developed calypso from Trinidad which became available through the early recordings and appearances of calypso troubadours such as "Lord Melody", "Brynner" and "Sparrow". Today, calypso and its derivative, soca, are the main forms produced and consumed by Antiguans. Over the years, the country has produced many artists who have had international impact, thus helping to shape and change the direction of calypso music. Paul "Obstinate" Richards, Rupert "Swallow" Philo and McLean "Short Shirt" Emmanuel are immortalised as creative pioneers. The national calypso competition, staged during the annual Carnival celebrations, has become the highlight of musical production and performance in the country. A final group of ten to twelve artists, chosen from an original field of up to one hundred singers, perform two songs each in annual competition against each other before thousands of excited fans. Ivena "Queen Ivena" Phillip became the first female to win the national calypso competition in 2003.

In recent years, the Party Monarch competition has been developed as a platform to highlight those artists whose main aim is to provide music for dancing/partying. This competition is highly favoured by the youth in

RIGHT
The legendary Mason Brothers Band make a rare appearance during the 50th anniversary celebrations of Carnival 2007.

FACING PAGE
The triumphant Hell's Gate Steelband celebrate their 2007 'Panorama' victory.
Photos: Joseph Jones

CLOCKWISE FROM TOP LEFT

One year after the first Carnival celebrations in 1957, Paul "Obstinate" Richards was crowned Calypso Monarch following his performances of 'Dance, Dance, Dance' and 'Obsti Will Sing Again'.

Veteran calypsonian Manroy "Creole" Hunte during the 50th anniversary celebrations of Carnival (1957-2007). He was first crowned Caribbean Calypso Monarch in 1967.

Performing during Carnival 2007, Rupert "Swallow" Philo first achieved success as Caribbean Calypso Monarch in 1973.

Ivena "Queen Ivena" Phillip entertains the crowds during Carnival 2007. She became the first female to win the Caribbean Calypso Monarch competition in 2003.

FACING PAGE
McLean "Short Shirt" Emmanuel was first crowned Caribbean Calypso Monarch in 1964. Since then he has been crowned many times and was again victorious during the 50th anniversary celebrations of Carnival 2007.
Photos: Joseph Jones

society and now rivals the national calypso competition as the cultural centre for musical excitement and pageantry.

Antigua has a fine tradition of orchestras and combos which provide music for all types of celebrations as well as entertainment within the country's tourism industry. Laviscount Brass, formed in the late fifties by John Laviscount, is still the leading band in the country. It retains the name of the founder although he has not been associated with the group for at least forty years. Other important groups were the bands of national cultural icon Oscar Mason (The

Vibratones and Sons of the Vibratones) along with the Ambrose Quintet, Gardner All Stars and the Saints Brothers. Smaller groups like the Entertainers (which featured Roland Prince who emerged as a world-rated jazz guitarist in the early seventies), the Targets, Teen Stars and Playboys, provided dance music for the youth of the 1960s and beyond. But, without doubt, the most successful musical group to come out of Antigua and Barbuda is the Burning Flames – a family unit (originally) that has dominated electronic music production since the early eighties. The group has performed around the

world with its eclectic mixture of voice, rhythm and melody capable of encouraging wild merriment and unhindered dancing.

The steelband, although introduced from Trinidad in the 1940s, had parallel development in Antigua and Barbuda and many 'firsts' for that twentieth century musical instrument were created by Antiguans; the most notable of which being the first steelband to be commercially recorded (Brute Force) is from Antigua. Pan competitions, all-girl steelbands, steelband associations and a number of specialised pan instruments evolved in Antigua even before

Trinidad. During the 1950s and 1960s, it was estimated that there was a steelband in every village and urban community. Among the best known was Hell's Gate Steelband (the first band formed in Antigua and the oldest steelband in the world), Red Army, North Star (which became Rising Sun) along with the modern bands like Supa Stars, Harmonites and Halcyon.

Steelband went through a period of decline in the late seventies but regained much of its popularity since the 1990s through the work of some of the pioneering stalwarts such as Eustace Manning Henry, the late Fundoo Bloodman and

TOP & LEFT
Gemonites Steel Orchestra in full flow during the 2007
'Panorama' contest.

ABOVE
Prime Minister Baldwin Spencer, left, presenting the
2007 'Panorama' trophy to Hell's Gate Steelband.
Photos: Joseph Jones

the younger, talented individuals such as Victor Babu Samuel, Patrick Stone Johnson and Lacu Samuel. The Gemonites Steelband organises an annual steelband festival which features many regional 'pannists' and small steelbands. The event is fast gaining international recognition.

After calypso, reggae music, in all its various manifestations, is perhaps the most important music in Antigua and Barbuda. Most bands and singers will perform all genres of music but reggae is particularly popular with regional and international visitors and residents alike. Choral singing, religious music and jazz are also popular forms of music. Keyboard players Winston Bailey, Rawdon Edwards and Dr George Roberts, and guitarist Roland Price, are perhaps the most important musicians contributing extensively to all these forms.

There is, however, a most curious phenomenon in Antigua and Barbuda: far from being only available on the radio, in music stores or at the various events, the best of the nation's musical talent can be experienced 'free of charge' in the many hotels, restaurants, nightclubs and casinos where they are employed in the service of the tourism industry.

Bountiful harvest provides unique gourmet experiences

SERENO BENJAMIN

When British planters were the only farmers in Antigua and Barbuda they cleared the island forest and planted sugarcane. Some people say that this is the reason why produce grown here has a "sugar in the land" taste.

The growing of fruit and vegetables and the rearing of livestock, is undertaken by small farmers throughout the country. They sell their produce through a Central Marketing Corporation, and organisation which contributes towards agricultural development and assists in the education of local farmers.

Producing food to satisfy the local demand, particularly the tourism sector, is one of the objectives of producers. Hotels and restaurants purchase locally-produced crops and livestock.

The production of fruit, vegetables, herbs, spices and cotton is unique in Antigua and Barbuda because of the dry, sunny climate. Fruit such as mango, finger rose (a type of banana), banana, sugar apple, citrus fruits, passions fruits, melons (water melon, cantaloupe and honey dew), papaya (pawpaw), pomegranate are among the popular fruits. Tamarind and avocado are also grown as well as gooseberry, cherries, sour-sop and plums (yellow and red).

There are many rare and little-known tropical fruits growing wild, including the 'sea grape' which, unlike grapes, do not grow on vines but on trees which are located on or near the beach. The 'gut apple' is found along streams and smells like a rose but has a bland taste. 'Macau' is a golf ball-sized fruit which grows on a palm tree but is not as plentiful as the date palm. Dates are usually available from coconut vendors who can be seen throughout the country. The 'monkey pear' is a burgundy-coloured fruit which is produced by a vining cactus and resembles the kiwi fruit, but unlike the kiwi, the flesh is white.

The prized fruit of the country is the Antigua 'black' pineapple, renowned over the world for its rich, sweet taste. This golden fruit is cultivated in the south of the island and has gained recognition among chefs and restaurateurs both locally and worldwide. Consequently, the government is supporting efforts to give the fruit a premium brand and offers incentives to encourage farmers to increase production.

RIGHT
Fruit and vegetables are produced and brought to market by small farmers.

FACING PAGE
The Antigua 'black' pineapple is world-renowned for its rich, sweet taste.

Photos: Joseph Jones

Market days are busy and colourful with a wide variety of produce on sale. Almost every type of fruit or vegetable can be bought including peas, corn, peppers (hot, seasoning and sweet), carrots, cucumbers, cabbages, lettuce, squash, pumpkin, beets, dasheen, cassava, yams and sweet potato. The sweet potato is one of the nation's most important root crops and is used in a wide variety of recipes including 'doucouna', a dish which reflects the country's African heritage. 'Bamboola', which is a bread made from cassava, is one of the most popular ways in which cassava is used, and during the Christmas period, yams become plentiful.

Spices and herbs such as allspice, citronella, rosemary, chive, thyme and basil are common ingredients in Antiguan food. The 'widdy-widdy' bush, is a herb that was brought over from west Africa. Lately, the use of plants and herbs in traditional medicine is gaining momentum as an alternative source of healing. Several thriving herbal gardens can be found around the island as a result of the recognition and important role herbs and spices play in local cuisine.

Although sugarcane is no longer grown for export, it is still produced by some farmers.

Another major crop which is important to the agricultural sector is West Indian sea island cotton. Antigua and Barbuda's Central Cotton Station is renowned for its role in maintaining the only gene bank of all types of the sea island cotton. Other countries that produce sea island cotton obtain their planting materials from Antigua and Barbuda.

Cattle, sheep and goats are the major livestock and are found grazing on pasture lands or roaming across the country.

Fishing is another important aspect of the agricultural industry. Sea food is becoming popular as both a healthy choice as well as a delicious alternative to meat products. Lobster, conch, shrimp and a range of fish dishes are popular in the home as well as on the restaurant menus.

The blend of cultural traditions and local foods, set against the backdrop of crystal-clear waters, sunny climate and spectacular beaches, make this little bit of paradise a unique and unforgettable experience.

A beach for every day of the year

RACHEL H. COLLIS

The tourism industry in Antigua and Barbuda accounts for approximately 85 percent of its foreign exchange earnings and employs around twenty percent of the workforce. The sector has seen significant growth in recent years, particularly in the areas of construction, where a number of public sector projects – such as the airport expansion – and a variety of private sector projects, have driven the expansion.

The additional tourism development initiatives are valued at over EC$1 billion and will benefit other sectors. These will, in turn, stimulate further growth in the country's economic output. The country is also undergoing a programme to improve its infrastructure. This includes road construction, repairs and maintenance across the state.

For many visitors, the airport is the first impression they get of Antigua and Barbuda. The V.C. Bird International Airport has undergone major improvements including

repainting, new air-conditioning systems, a refurbished and extended VIP lounge, a new canopy to the front of the terminal and the construction of a new upper level departure lounge. To meet stringent international security requirements, new security screens have been installed along with the addition of new emigration and immigration booths to reduce passenger-processing times.

A little over 250,000 tourists arrive by air each year with the majority coming from the United Kingdom and the United States. However, cruise tourism has enjoyed steady growth in recent years with more than four hundred ships sailing into the four-birth dock in St John's annually. Passenger numbers are now in excess of 600,000. While the increased competition from other cruise destinations may have an impact on the region, Antigua and Barbuda is expected to maintain its market share and reputation as a destination offering "safer waters".

ABOVE
Souvenir steelpans.
Photo: Joseph Jones

RIGHT
Named 'Hotel of the Year, 2005' by the *Tatler* Travel Guide, Carlisle Bay is a stunning addition to Antigua's diverse hotel sector. With its dramatic backdrop of rolling hills and tropical rainforest, the hotel's contemporary design is impressive. It offers a wide range of facilities including two restaurants, a health spa, nine tennis courts and a small movie theatre.

FACING PAGE
Dickenson Bay – where the beach is just the beginning.
Photo: Joseph Jones

CLOCKWISE FROM TOP

Cruise tourism has enjoyed steady growth with more than four hundred ships sailing into the four-birth dock in St John's every year.
Photo: Joseph Jones

With its own private bay and set within fourteen acres of tropical gardens, Blue Waters is one of Antigua's most secluded tropical resorts. Established in the early 1970s, the hotel offers a choice of luxury rooms, suites and villas, a spa, gym, tennis court and two restaurants.

Annual cruise ship passenger numbers are in excess of 600,000, and Heritage Quay is their first port of call.
Photo: Joseph Jones

Antigua and Barbuda is one of the pioneers of yachting in the Caribbean. Its reputation is known throughout the world as a destination of choice for many international yachtsmen. Annual events such as the Classic Yacht Regatta and the exhilarating Stanford Antigua Sailing Week have added a new dimension to the country's status as a traditional Caribbean destination.

Carnival in Antigua and Barbuda is another attraction. It has become one of the Caribbean's greatest summer festivals and celebrated its 50th anniversary in 2007.

The white-sand beach is the first image that comes to mind when one thinks of a Caribbean holiday destination. Antigua and Barbuda is blessed with 365, including Barbuda's miles of deserted beaches and its pink sands. Although these treasures occur naturally, their protection and enhancement is a firm commitment of the government. With the help of UNESCO, it has established recommended distances from the shore where buildings should not be erected. This simple but effective rule offers protection to the beachfront and its indigenous wildlife.

CLOCKWISE FROM TOP

The 'Black Swan' runs pirate-themed party cruises around the island.
Photo: Joseph Jones

Located at Johnsons Point on Antigua's west coast, Turner's Beach Bar & Grill is a popular hang-out for tourists and locals.
Photo: Joseph Jones

Nestled within gardens overlooking Nelson's Dockyard, Ocean Inn provides a combination of luxury, history and tropical elegance.

Established by renowned Antiguan yachtsman Hugh Bailey and his family in 1968, the Catamaran Hotel is a truly Caribbean inn. Located at Falmouth Harbour near Nelson's Dockyard, the hotel is a popular choice for couples and families.

FACING PAGE
'Coral Ark' offers party cruises from St John's.
Photo: Joseph Jones

CLOCKWISE FROM TOP

With its luxurious accommodation, Jumby Bay is one of the most exclusive resorts in Antigua and Barbuda. Surrounded by lush, tropical foliage and pristine white-sand beaches, it is located on the privately-owned Long Island, which lies two miles off the north-east coast of Antigua.

Long Bay Hotel has been operated by the Lafaurie family since 1966 and is situated on a peninsula with a quiet bay on one side and a beautiful beach on the other. Comprising bay-side rooms and secluded cottages, the hotel offers fine dining, watersports and a championship tennis court.

A relaxing, poolside massage is all part of the service at Dian Bay Resort & Spa. Set within lush tropical gardens, this secluded, hillside resort offers spectacular views of the lagoon and sea.

Located between St John's and V.C. Bird International Airport, the Amaryllis Hotel offers a friendly and relaxed atmosphere.

Trade Winds Hotel is situated on a hillside overlooking the spectacular Dickenson Bay. Set within lush, landscaped gardens, the hotel has an unhurried and welcoming environment.

FACING PAGE
Hobie cats wait to be taken out to sea by guests at Sandals Hotel.
Photo: Joseph Jones

ABOVE
The distinctive Curtain Bluff resort has been in operation since 1962. Situated on the Curtain Bluff peninsula at the southern tip of Antigua, it is ideally positioned for unrivalled views of the Caribbean Sea.
Photo: K Maguire

LEFT
Tying the knot in Antigua has been the destination of choice for many couples throughout the world. Organising the ceremony and obtaining a marriage licence is an uncomplicated affair.
Photo: Joseph Martin

FACING PAGE
Watching the boats sail by from a shaded hammock must seem like paradise on earth.
Photo: Joseph Jones

An unspoilt island paradise

VENETA BURTON

Barbuda is the sister island of Antigua and lies 28 miles to the north. It is 62 square miles or about fourteen miles by eight miles in size with a population of approximately 1500. The island is, largely, flat - with a high point of 125 ft - and is one of the few remaining unspoilt islands in the Caribbean. Barbuda can be reached in fifteen minutes by air or one hour and thirty minutes by ferry service from Antigua.

The original inhabitants were the Arawaks and the Caribs and they called it Wa'Omoni, meaning "land of the herons". After 1493, the Spanish named the island "Barbuda" because of its 'bearded' appearance due to its forested landscape. It is said that in 1628, settlers from St Kitts called it "Dulcina" because of its pleasantness.

Codrington is the only village on Barbuda and was named after Christopher Codrington who, in 1685, leased the island for 185 years. The boundaries of Codrington were set by the British town and country planners. They experimented with the idea of planning a city by dividing living spaces into rectangles. To the west, the lagoon marked one boundary; the north by Sedge Garden; the east by Indigo; and the south by the Park. Barbuda's historical sites include Martello Tower (or River Fort) which is a lookout post that was built to defend the main anchorage. Another historical site is Highland House, although it is known locally as "Willybob". The Codrington family built the house sometime after 1720 on the highlands of Barbuda.

One of the world's largest nesting colonies of the magnificent frigate bird is located in Barbuda. The island is also home to several caves and sink holes including Bryant, Darby, Indian and Dark cave. It is within these caves that visitors may view ancient petroglyphs (rock carvings) made by the island's earliest inhabitants, the Amerindians.

Barbuda is also known for its shipwrecks. With more than 147 sites located off its coastline, it is a scuba-diver's paradise. The island is a favourite destination for the rich and famous who are drawn to its miles of deserted beaches, tranquil blue waters and peaceful environment.

RIGHT
The journey to school in Codrington.

FACING PAGE
A little shade on the beach at Low Bay.
Photos: Joseph Jones

TOP & RIGHT
The rugged landscape around Two Foot Bay is pock-marked with many caves and potholes.
Photos: Joseph Jones

ABOVE
The airstrip near Codrington is one of two landing sites for small aircraft arriving in Barbuda.
Photo: Antigua and Barbuda Tourism Department

FACING PAGE
Located near River Beach in the south of Barbuda, the Martello Tower was built onto a pre-existing fort in the early 19th century. Its purpose was to defend the south-western coast of the island.
Photo: Joseph Jones

Codrington Lagoon occupies most of the western region of Barbuda. The town of Codrington is located on its eastern shore and it is separated from the Caribbean Sea by a thin stretch of land.
Photo: Joseph Jones

TOP
Two Foot Bay, on Barbuda's northern shore, is where rocks and crags sit side-by-side with white-sand beaches.
Photo: Joseph Jones

LEFT
The Caribbean Sea and Codrington Lagoon are separated by a stretch of land that forms most of the western coastline of Barbuda.
Photo: Ann Granger

FACING PAGE
The 'pink' beaches at Palmetto Point derive their colour from the deposits of coloured shells that are washed upon the shore.
Photo: Joseph Jones

Palm Beach, at Low Bay,
is a staggering fourteen-
mile stretch of beach along
Barbuda's western coast.

Photo: Joseph Jones

The sporting challenge of the open sea

RODDY GRIMES-GRAEME

Sailing is at the core of Antigua and Barbuda, as it has been since the arrival of the first settlers. It was the mode of transport that brought Amerindians to the islands as they made their way up the Caribbean island chain from the South American mainland. Their simple canoes, with rudimentary sails, carried these early settlers throughout the waters of the Caribbean.

Christopher Columbus, in turn, would arrive by sail in the late 1400s, bringing the first Europeans to the region. And from the 1500s to the 1800s, the shipping lanes were busy with the naval ships of battling European colonisers; merchant ships carrying away the precious and bountiful resources of the Caribbean; pirates and privateers; and ships packed with their human cargoes of enslaved Africans.

The geographic position at the upwind, northeast corner of the Leeward Islands made Antigua an ideal location for the British Navy to establish a base from which to protect the British colonies. And its largely central position in the Caribbean island chain afforded good access to the other islands.

Antigua is still a natural point of entry for sailing vessels coming into the Caribbean. A significant industry has developed in the remains of the British Navy's Georgian base at Nelson's Dockyard where Commander Nicholson and his family arrived after the Second World War on their schooner 'Mollihawk' and helped found what is now the worldwide charter yachting industry. They began restoring the dockyard, one of the Caribbean's best natural harbours and 'hurricane holes', and set out to charter Mollihawk to wealthy guests on trips to other unspoiled islands.

Today, yachts of all sizes converge on Antigua from all over the world to enjoy the favourable and sometimes challenging sailing

RIGHT & FACING PAGE
Antigua Sailing Week
South Coast Race.

Photos: Joseph Jones

Antigua Sailing Week
South Coast Race.
Photo: Joseph Jones

conditions. Everything from dinghies and small sailboats to the enormous motor yachts and cruisers line the docks and quays of English Harbour and Falmouth Harbour. All of them are tended to by excellent local services as part of a large and flourishing yachting industry. This industry now includes locally-built boats and small classic yachts. Most yachtsmen, both professional and amateur, list the island as a favourite place from which to operate in the winter season because of its unmatched services, conditions, harbours and beaches. And its upwind location still means that many excellent cruising destinations are just a day or two's sail away. It's so ideal, in fact, that many sailors have made homes here after spending seasons in Antigua.

In 1967, a group of yachtsmen, including Commander Nicholson's son Desmond, held an informal regatta at the end of the winter charter season. That first event heralded the arrival of Antigua Sailing Week and was won by Dr Cesar Barrios of Puerto Rico in his 38 ft 'Enzian'. Since then, the occasion has grown into one of the world's top sailing events. Many also know it as one of the sailing world's great party weeks where the shore-side atmosphere is fuelled largely by local rum, music and dance.

Today, the competition attracts more than two hundred yachts racing over five days in eight classes, and attended by thousands of crew-members, spectators and revellers. The fleet is split into Racing and Cruising divisions to keep accidents to a minimum and to offer challenging courses to all participants. The cruisers run shorter courses but often enjoy closer racing as the boats are more closely matched in speed. There is a large 'bareboat' contingent in the cruising division; these are yachts crewed by

Antigua Sailing Week
South Coast Race.

Photo: Joseph Jones

people who share the cost of a charter and all race together. They are also known to party the hardest! The racers take the event more seriously. Reputations are at stake as some of the world's finest boats compete on the lively Trade Wind courses. The waters around Antigua and Barbuda are also known for 'great wind' and big waves, which make the racing conditions spectacular; with bright spinnakers floating over deep blue water and fast yachts surfing down long swells.

That first regatta in 1968 consisted mainly of yachts that would be considered 'classic' or vintage, even by the standards of the day. Such yachts had their own class until 1988 when Captain Kenny and Jane Coombs founded their own event – the Antigua Classic Yacht Regatta. It occurs in the week before Race Week and is smaller, quieter and far less rowdy, but it is one of the world's most beautiful sights as up to sixty yachts, some over 100 years old, glide by on acres of sail. Lest you think these ancient

ABOVE
Antigua Classic
Yacht Regatta.

FACING PAGE
Antigua Sailing Week
South Coast Race.

Photos: Joseph Jones

Antigua Classic
Yacht Regatta.

Photo: Joseph Jones

boats are pampered, this regatta is known as the place where these extraordinary craft are pushed harder than any other. It has even been a catalyst for the development of 'modern classics' – new yachts that are built to look old. Indeed, some of the spectacular 120 ft, J-class yachts that contested the Americas Cup in the 1930s (one of which is a modern replica), met here for the first time in seventy years. The entire Classic yachting world looks forward to this regatta with great anticipation; some spend the whole year preparing for the event.

Antigua and Barbuda also has a long tradition of developing excellent local sailors at nearly every level of the sport. Karl James is a top Caribbean Laser class sailor and is a two-time Olympian. Laser is one of the smallest and simplest dinghies but is one of the world's largest and most competitive classes. It has launched many of the best-known racing careers in the past few decades.

Karl runs the Antigua Yacht Club's dinghy program and gives many local youths the chance to train with a champion.

Antiguan yachts place well at nearly every Caribbean regatta and there is a very keen rivalry with St Maarten. Shannon Falcone is another local sailor. He competed in the 2003 and 2007 Americas Cup Regattas, the very pinnacle of the sport. Antiguans Eli Fuller, Inigo Ross and Ty Brodie also represented the nation at the Olympics in the windsurfing class. Andre Phillip is one of the world's top kite-surfers and that sport constantly looks to him for style and inspiration. Many more Antiguans and Barbudans make a living from yachting, either as crew or in the many support industries that surround the yachts. It all serves to make the English Harbour area one of the most vibrant parts of the island and it is well worth a visit to see some truly spectacular vessels and soak up the lively yachting culture.

A new chapter in the history of Antigua Sailing Week

The sailors and vessels that have distinguished themselves during Antigua Sailing Week since 1967 are a veritable *Who's Who* in the sport of yacht racing. The names are legendary: Desmond Nicholson, Jolyon Byerly, Don Street, Tom Hill, Robin Tatersall, Peter Holmberg and Roy Disney. And the yachts are equally well known: 'Titan', 'Kialoa', 'Infinity', 'Sayonara', 'Morning Glory' and 'Pyewacket'.

As this world-class competition entered its 40th anniversary year in 2007, it did so with a new title sponsor – Stanford International Bank Ltd.

It was in 1967 that yacht broker Desmond Nicholson and Antiguan hotelier Howard Hulford came up with the idea of a spring regatta. This first race was around Barbuda and included ten entrants; it marked the birth of Antigua Sailing Week. The following year, the two pioneers joined forces with Ed Sheerin and Peter Deeth and a larger event was organised. It included the yachts 'Lord Jim', 'Escapade', 'Royono', 'Veleda', 'Eilean', 'Thamilla', 'Enzian', 'Jibaro' and 'Iolaire', which set out from English Harbour to sail in a three-day event.

The overall winner that year (and the following year) was the Puerto Rican crew aboard Dr Caesar Barrios' 'Enzian'. Barrios was returning home after a cruise to Grenada and participated in the event by chance. "He was passing through Antigua and was dragged into the event," recalled Antiguan sailing legend Jolyon Byerley. "It was probably the best thing that could have happened as word of this friendly little regatta spread through the northern islands. In fact, the first three years were won by Puerto Rican boats, as 'Enzian's' success was followed by Dick Doran in 'Laughing Sally', said Byerley.

The following year, Bob Thompson, of the US Virgin Islands, took the overall position in 'I'll Do'. Jolyon Byerley, himself, went on to win the 1972 regatta with 'Matchless', and the 1973 event aboard 'Sundance'.

By 1974, the fleet had grown to 52 entries in four divisions. Among those was the famous television chef Graham Kerr ("The Galloping Gourmet") in 'Treena'. But the boat that grabbed the headlines was 'Supercilious' which was owned by another Englishman, Tony Lawson. With Don "Squeaky" Street at the helm and with an all-star crew including Peter Bowker and Peter Vandersloot, "Super C" put on a sailing master-class in the heavy-air conditions and easily outdistanced its competitors.

In 1975, yet another talented Puerto Rican sailed into the winner's circle. Tom Hill's lively 'Titan' was the top vessel in the 60-boat fleet that year. This was the first of four Antigua Sailing Week victories for Hill. In 1987 and 1990, he won with 'Titan 4', and in 2005 he was victorious with the powerful 'Titan XII'.

Joining the likes of Berrios, Byerley and Hill, there have been many sailors who managed to overcome the odds and win the week's overall prize on multiple occasions. Virgin Islands superstar, Peter Holmberg managed it in 1985, 1986 and 1992. So, too, has John Thomson, with 'Infinity', in 1988, 1989 and 1996. Another three-time winner is software mogul and America's Cup campaigner, Larry Ellison whose 'Sayonara' won back-to-back events in 1997 and 1998, then again in 2000. Two-time Antigua Sailing Week champions include John Foster in 1980 and 1981 with 'Antidote'; Jim Kilroy, skipper of the famed 'Kialoa' in 1982 and 1983; and Dr Hasso Plattner in 2001 and 2004 with two different yachts called 'Morning Glory'.

And it is not just the winners who have made Antigua Sailing Week the leading regatta in the Caribbean and one of the world's top five sailing events. The high quality of the boats, and the skills of all the captains and crews play their part in this popular and exiting competition.

More information on Stanford Antigua Sailing Week can be found at www.sailingweek.com.

FACING PAGE
'Chippewa' is put through its paces during Stanford Antigua Sailing Week in 2007.

Photo: Matteo Torres / Stanford International Bank

Vibrant capital city steeped in history and tradition

SIR JAMES CARLISLE

The capital city of St John's was the first city in the British West Indies to be laid out in the grid system. Since its establishment, it has undergone many changes, although some have been the result of natural disasters such as hurricanes and earthquakes.

Over recent years, the city has developed into a world class financial hub as well as an attractive and popular duty free shopping location. Traditional Caribbean markets sit alongside exclusive boutiques which create a bustling and vibrant atmosphere. Amid this busy environment, many historic landmarks and buildings provide a constant reminder of the nation's past as well as a celebration of its heroes.

Built by Nathaniel Gilbert, the man responsible for developing Methodism in Antigua, the Ebenezer Methodist Church is located on St Mary's Street and is the spiritual home of Methodism in Antigua and Barbuda.

The Old Court House, which was built in 1750, was badly damaged in the earthquake of 1974 and is now home to the Museum of Antigua and Barbuda.

Coates Cottage on Lower Nevis Street is the home of one of the country's leading art galleries. However, the building's past is considerably more sinister because it was once a barracoon – an enclosure used for the confinement of slaves or convicts.

The Cenotaph, which is situated at the junction of High Street and Independence Avenue, is a memorial to the men who died during the First World War (1914-18) and the Second World War (1939-45).

The Westerby Monument was erected in honour of Bishop Westerby of the Moravian Church who was instrumental in providing education for former slaves and for improving the water supply in St John's.

The Prince Klaas (King Court) Monument was erected in honour of Prince Klaas (King Court) who was the leader of the slave rebellion of 1736. Betrayed by a fellow slave, most of the conspirators were tortured and then executed.

The statue of the Rt Hon Sir Vere Cornwall Bird is situated in Market Square. This monument honours the 'Father of the Nation'

RIGHT
Centrally located in Market Square, the statue of Sir Vere Cornwall Bird is one of the capital's most distinctive landmarks.

FACING PAGE
St John's Cathedral is an imposing building that dominates the capital's skyline. Built in the mid-1840s, on the site of two previous Anglican churches (circa 1681 & 1720), it came into service in 1847 and was consecrated in 1848.

Photos: Joseph Jones

CLOCKWISE FROM TOP

The period architecture of Redcliffe Quay.

The sidewalks of Corn Alley.

City View Hotel.

Photos: Joseph Jones

who became the first Chief Minister on 1 January 1960; the first Premier on 27 February 1967; and the first Prime Minister on 1 November 1981.

Dominating the capital's skyline is St John's Cathedral. This imposing building was opened for service in 1847 and consecrated in 1848. The cathedral is the third Anglican structure to occupy the site. The first church was built of wood and was erected in 1681; in 1720, it was replaced by a brick-built church.

Government House is a colonial, Georgian building which is the official seat of the Governor-General. The Emancipation document was signed here in 1834.

The Antigua Recreation Ground (ARG) has been the home of cricket in Antigua and Barbuda for more that twenty-five years. It was here, in 1994, that Brian Lara scored 375 runs to break the record of 365 runs held by Sir Garfield Sobers. Lara's record was broken by Matthew Hayden in 2003, but was broken again by Lara at the ARG in 2004 with 400 runs.

The original Parliament Building, on Parliament Drive, was erected in 1981 when Antigua and Barbuda achieved independence from Great Britain. It was opened by HRH Princess Margaret on 2 November 1981. In 2006, a new Parliament Building was constructed and was opened by HRH Prince Edward on 30 October 2006. It is situated on Queen Elizabeth Highway adjacent to the Prime Minister's Office.

CLOCKWISE FROM TOP

'Cruise ship day' in the capital.

The Westerby Monument honours Bishop Westerby who helped to provide education for former slaves.

The West Bus Terminal.

FACING PAGE
Fishing boats docked at Fisherman's Wharf.

Photos: Joseph Jones

ABOVE
A fine example of traditional Caribbean architecture.

RIGHT
Built in 1750, and owned by a well known merchant, the building now known as Government House was acquired in 1800 by the British Government as a residence for the Governor of the Leeward Islands. Since then it has been the official residence of the Governors and Governors-General of Antigua and Barbuda.

BOTTOM RIGHT
The strikingly decorated Joe Mike's Hotel is located in the heart of the capital.

FACING PAGE
The Public Market Complex is a daily hive of activity.

Photos: Joseph Jones

CLOCKWISE FROM TOP

The Ebenezer Methodist Church is the spiritual home of Methodism in Antigua and Barbuda.

The Prince Klaas Monument honours one of the country's national heroes.

Covered walkways and traditional architecture add a quintessentially Caribbean feel to the shopping experience.

FACING PAGE
The Cenotaph commemorates those who fell during the First and Second World Wars.

Photos: Joseph Jones

Northerly view across the
capital and harbour looking
towards Runaway Bay.
Photo: Photogenesis

Bright economic future plus excellent investment opportunities

RASONA DAVIS & KEVIN SILSTON

Since gaining independence from Britain in 1981, Antigua and Barbuda has transformed itself from an agrarian economy to a service-driven, upper middle-income economy with annual per capita income of over US$ 10,000. Tourism is the mainstay of the economy, contributing directly and indirectly to over 60 percent of gross domestic product (GDP). The country is a premier tourist destination and has received many accolades for high quality services. These include *Caribbean World International* magazine's 'Best Wedding Island of the Year' award in 2005 and 2006. Antigua and Barbuda is also among the top five wedding and honeymoon destinations as ranked by American Express and was deemed the 'Best Beach Destination' by Expedia.com. With strong performance of the tourism sector along with growth in other sectors such as construction, communications, banking and insurance and other services, Antigua and Barbuda has experienced real economic growth averaging 5.0 percent per annum over the past twenty-five years.

In addition to its strong growth and high per capita income, Antigua and Barbuda boasts high social development indicators with impressive performance in respect of life expectancy, literacy and infant mortality rates. These outcomes were made possible through the provision of universal primary education and health care services. The United Nations Human Development Report for 2006 lists Antigua and Barbuda as one of the countries with high human development. These high levels of economic and social development were achieved in spite of the significant challenges posed by the country's vulnerability to external economic shocks and natural disasters.

In the 1980s, real economic growth averaged 7.0 percent annually due to significant public and private sector investments, particularly in the tourism industry. From the early 1990s, Antigua and Barbuda faced the devastation of a number of hurricanes and tropical storms and suffered economic losses due to world economic recessions and globalisation. These shocks resulted in a slowdown in economic growth to an average of 3.0 percent between the early

RIGHT
The Deep Water Harbour in St John's is the hub for cruise liners and container ships.

FACING PAGE
Opened in 1987, the Heritage Hotel (foreground) is located at Heritage Quay, in the capital, and is ideal for tourists and business people alike. It is surrounded by a variety of duty free shops, stores and restaurants and is next to the popular Vendors Mall. The hotel offers spacious and well-appointed executive rooms and suites as well as fully-equipped conference facilities.

Photos: Joseph Jones

1990s and the early 2000s. The slowdown in economy activity was further compounded by the tragic events of 9/11 which resulted in the country recording economic growth of 1.5 percent. By 2003, economic performance rebounded significantly with output increasing by 4.3 percent. For the three-year period 2003 to 2005 real GDP grew by an average of 5.0 percent driven by the expansion of economic activity in the construction sector (9.6 percent) and the tourism industry (5.3 percent).

Economic activity in Antigua and Barbuda grew by 12.2 percent in 2006 compared with an increase of 5.5 percent in 2005, primarily fuelled by developments in construction and supported by tourism. All sectors recorded growth in 2006 but activity in the construction sector continued to provide the impetus for growth with a record increase of 35.0 percent, which follows growth of 19.5 percent in 2005. The remarkable performance in this sector was driven by developments in both the public and private

sectors largely associated with Cricket World Cup (CWC) 2007. Public sector activity focused on construction of the Sir Vivian Richards Cricket Stadium, road works and other infrastructural development projects. Further, over $700 million was invested by private sector companies to undertake the construction and expansion of a number of hotels, condominiums and guesthouses. There was also an appreciable expansion in residential construction marked by increased commercial bank credit to households for home construction and renovation.

Tourism activity, as measured by value-added in the hotels and restaurants sector, grew by 2.5 percent in 2006 with total visitor arrivals increasing to 742,168. Of this, 253,669 represent stay-over visitors, which rose by 3.4 percent. Stay-over arrivals from the United States increased by 7.1 percent; partly reflecting additional airlift from Delta Airlines and increased marketing initiatives in traditional and

135

CLOCKWISE FROM TOP

This state-of-the-art power station generates 51 megawatts of electricity and is a joint venture between Antigua Power Company Ltd and the Antigua Public Utilities Authority.

For more than thirty years, West Indies Oil Company Ltd has been supplying oils, gas, lubricants and LPG to the people of Antigua and Barbuda. The company operates several 24-hour service stations as well as specialising in the supply of LPG for homes and hotels. It also offers bunker fuels for boats and a waste oil collection service.

Antigua Computer Technology Co. Ltd (ACT) was established in 1989 and employs more than fifty people. It is the leading single-source technology provider in Antigua and Barbuda and supplies a wide range of users including schools, government establishments, hotels and financial institutions.

Located at the Woods Shopping Centre in St John's, Ortho Medical Associates is a state-of-the-art medical facility providing a wide range of services including orthopaedic surgery, addiction medicine, general medical practice, physical therapy and radiology. It is one of the most advanced speciality clinics in the Eastern Caribbean.

non-traditional markets. The tourism product was re-branded, and some hotels offered special romantic packages during the summer months, which further boosted the level of arrivals. The level of arrivals from non-traditional markets increased along with arrivals from traditional markets. In particular, arrivals from Germany increased by 13.6 percent while arrivals from France and the Caribbean grew by 11.6 percent and 11.5 percent respectively.

Other economic sectors also experienced strong growth in 2006. These include mining and quarrying, the transport sector, banks and insurance, government services and the communications sector.

Economic growth in Antigua and Barbuda has been supported by a strong and stable exchange rate and historically low inflation. The Eastern Caribbean dollar has been pegged to the US dollar (EC$ 2.70 = US$ 1.00) since 1976. Despite the volatility in crude oil prices, inflation has remained low, averaging between 2 to 2.5 percent. Also, unemployment is relatively low – the unemployment rate for 2006 was estimated at 4.4 percent.

On the external accounts, Antigua and Barbuda maintained a balance of payments surplus between 2001 and 2005. Though the country is a net importer, its current account deficits are fully financed by large surpluses on the capital and financial account which are driven by significant foreign direct investment flows; for the period 2001 to 2005, these amounted to about US$ 600 m.

The provision of international financial services in Antigua and Barbuda has proven to be economically viable and has demonstrated

The 500-acre development at Jolly Harbour includes an 18-hole championship golf course, full service marina, shopping centre, restaurants and bars, villa rentals and sales, a wide range of sports facilities and spectacular white-sand beaches.

Photo: Joseph Jones

FROM TOP LEFT

As its name suggests, The Map Shop specialises in the sale of maps, charts, prints and travel guides of the Caribbean. Located in St John's, it also offers a wide range of books including many by Caribbean authors and publishers.

The Chairman and CEO of Global Bank of Commerce, Brian Stuart-Young, was named 'Global Banker of the Year 2007' by the prestigious *World Finance* magazine.

Located in Redcliffe Street in St John's, Best of Books is Antigua and Barbuda's largest and most comprehensive bookshop. With weekly shipments from the United Kingdom and the United States, the range of books on offer is diverse and extensive. The store also carries a wide selection of locally-produced souvenirs, arts and crafts and prints.

FACING PAGE

Agriculture accounts for approximately 4.5 percent of GDP. These farmers, at Cades Bay, are harvesting the Antigua 'black' pineapple, one of the most lucrative crops.

Photo: Joseph Jones

the potential to generate significant revenues and employment. The international financial services sector originated with the enactment of the International Business Corporation Act in 1982. The sector has grown significantly and offers a wide range of products, including a Registry of International Business Corporations, International Banking, International Trust Corporations, a Ship Registry, and Interactive Gaming and Interactive Wagering. The financial services sector in Antigua and Barbuda is well regulated by the Financial Services Regulatory Commission (FSRC) in collaboration with the Office of National Drug and Money Laundering Control Policy (ONDCP). Together, these agencies aim to maintain the integrity of the jurisdiction and to facilitate adherence to

international best practices. At the same time confidentiality remains paramount and, as such, specific procedures and mechanisms exist in order to safeguard the privacy and discretion enshrined in the legislation under which the international businesses operate.

In order to take advantage of new opportunities in the sector Antigua and Barbuda will soon introduce new products that will secure the country as the pre-eminent jurisdiction for asset protection and wealth management. These new products will be supported by the appropriate legislation which seeks to strengthen confidentiality and offer a greater degree of protection to clients. The new laws are the International Trust Act, the International Foundation Act, the International Limited

Liability Company Act; and the Company Management and Trust Service Providers Act.

Antigua and Barbuda was among the first jurisdictions to license interactive gaming and wagering companies. The island is known as the premier Internet gaming jurisdiction and has proven its capacity for innovation, adherence to international standards and protection of its customers. This sector generated significant revenues and employment for locals and had the potential to be a viable economic alternative for the country. However, the sector has been adversely affected by the ban imposed by the United States on Internet gaming. Over the past few years Antigua and Barbuda has been engaged in a cross border Internet gaming dispute with the US. With its limited resources and financial challenges, this tiny nation successfully challenged the US at several levels of the World Trade Organisation's dispute settlement system. However, instead of complying the US continues to pursue

protectionist stances, the latest being an announcement to withdraw its commitments under the General Agreement on Trade in Services (GATS) in respect of internet gaming. This ongoing dispute continues to impede the development of the sector and places immense financial and other pressures on Antigua and Barbuda as it seeks to traverse the dispute settlement mechanism of the WTO.

In the World Bank's report entitled 'Doing Business 2007', which assesses the regulations that impact business activity in countries, Antigua and Barbuda was ranked 33rd out of 175 developing and developed nations. This outcome reflects the existence of a business-friendly atmosphere where investors, whether local or foreign, can conduct their business efficiently. Antigua and Barbuda boasts an impressive assortment of service providers that can meet every business need. These service providers include attorneys, accountants, various domestic and international financial institutions,

real estate agents, software providers and Internet service providers. In addition, the country offers state-of-the-art and affordable telecommunications infrastructure along with reliable utilities and other ancillary services.

To ensure that Antigua and Barbuda continues to experience high and sustainable growth and encourages investment by local, regional and international investors, the government, under the leadership of Prime Minister Baldwin Spencer, is currently implementing a comprehensive reform programme. Specific focus has been on reducing the level of bureaucracy, simplifying the tax system, enhancing efficiency in the public sector and establishing appropriate institutions to support investment and private sector initiatives. The

overall objectives of the reform process include creating a stable macroeconomic environment, ensuring the existence of strong and efficient institutions and cultivating an enabling environment for private sector-led growth.

At the centre of the government's strategy to facilitate the investment and encourage private sector development is the Antigua and Barbuda Investment Authority (ABIA). To facilitate the establishment and operation of the Investment Authority, the Antigua and Barbuda Investment Authority Act and the Antigua and Barbuda Investment Code were enacted. The Investment Authority, which commenced operations in May 2007, provides a focused and co-ordinated mechanism for the promotion and facilitation of investment.

It is a one-stop-shop that guides investors wishing to start-up business in Antigua and Barbuda, assists in explaining investment incentives and provides support services for all investors. With the establishment of the ABIA, the granting of concessions to all categories of investors will no longer be discretionary. Investors will be granted incentives based on the viability of their projects and the projects' compatibility with the economic and developmental objectives of Antigua and Barbuda.

The Investment Code ensures greater transparency in the granting of concessions, provides full protection and security to investors in accordance with international standards, spells out the incentives and concessions to which investors are entitled and makes provisions for dispute settlement and compensation for losses.

In setting up the ABIA, it was also recognised the need to make special provisions for micro and small businesses to ensure that they are adequately equipped to take advantage of the concessions and incentives packages. As

TOP
The busy concourse at V.C. Bird International Airport.

LEFT
The ACB Financial Centre is a high-tech, state-of-the-art complex in St John's.
Photos: Joseph Jones

TOP
Handling almost one million arrivals and departures every year, V.C. Bird International Airport has become one of the Caribbean's leading airports.
Photo: Joseph Martin

RIGHT
Considered to be a true Caribbean institution, LIAT has been serving the region for fifty years. The Caribbean airline has a network of destinations that stretches from the Dominican Republic in the north to Guyana in the south. This popular carrier is the airline of choice for connecting the entire Caribbean.

such, the ABIA has been charged with providing support and technical assistance to micro and small businesses in areas such as productivity enhancement and business and financial planning. To increase the ability of small businesses to access credit, the government collaborated with the Stanford Group of Companies to establish the Empowerment for Ownership Initiative which has the objective of promoting the formulation of successful, independent businesses. To facilitate this, the Stanford Group of Companies has made $10 million available for the provision of concessionary loans to micro and small businesses. Since its launch in August 2005, this initiative has facilitated the expansion and development of over 140 micro and small businesses by providing over $5 million in credit to local entrepreneurs.

Economic activity is projected to expand by 3.0 percent in 2007, with developments in tourism and the other services driving the growth process. Indications are that stay-over arrivals will grow based on an increase in the

number of hotel rooms, additional airlift from the US and the UK, and continued marketing thrust in the US and western Europe. Activity in the construction sector is expected to remain robust over the medium term with significant private sector investment in major hotel and other projects such as the construction of the new medical school. Consistent with the expected developments in tourism and construction growth in value added is also forecasted for the transport, wholesale and retail, communication and banking and insurance sectors.

Growth in GDP is projected to converge to its long-run growth path of approximately 3.5 percent per annum in the medium term. However, there may be an upward shift in the long-run growth path resulting from significant investments in infrastructure, particularly the airport and continued enhancement of the quality and capacity of the country's tourism plant, improved marketing initiatives and the overall pursuit of policies that encourage investment and promote private sector development. Overall, Antigua and Barbuda faces a bright economic future, is well positioned as an idyllic vacation destination and, with its focus on facilitating business, offers excellent investment opportunities.

TOP
Abbott's Jewellery & Perfumery is located in the heart of the Heritage Quay Duty Free Mall in St John's. It provides a wide selection of jewellery, watches, china, crystal, fragrances and a host of fine gifts and accessories. This Antiguan-owned business is an authorised dealer for many leading brands including Rolex, Cartier, Breitling, Omega, Rado, Tag Heuer, Gucci, Raymond Weil and Movado.

LEFT
Shoul's Toys, Gifts & Houseware is located in the heart of St John's and is one of the largest and longest established businesses in Antigua. It is one of the most popular shopping centres in the capital and is also a household name throughout the country. The store's Christmas decorations (pictured) are a highlight of the festive season.

ABOVE
The head offices of ABI
Financial Group are at the
heart of downtown St John's.

Leading the way in financial services

Branded with positively moving coloured arrows, that depict their diversity and forward momentum, the entities comprising the ABI Financial Group (ABI) continue to make bold moves and grow beyond the shores of Antigua and Barbuda.

Indigenous to the twin-island nation, the group's network of affiliated companies exemplifies the country's national motto, "Each endeavouring, all achieving", by combining enterprise and effort to provide professional financial services that positively impact individuals and economies locally, regionally and internationally.

The ABI Financial Centre on Redcliffe Street in St John's, is the headquarters of the group and its entities: ABI Bank Ltd, Antigua Overseas Bank Ltd, ABI Trust Ltd, ABI Insurance Company Ltd, ABI Development Company Ltd, ASD Financial Services Corporation, Jolly Beach Resort, and Jolly Beach Vacations. The companies offer a wide variety of products and services ranging from domestic banking, international private banking, company formation, investment, corporate and trust services, brokerage services and wealth management to insurance, real estate development and resort management. The Financial Group is managed by a team of professional executives with a wealth of experience in all its areas of service.

ABI stays true to its core values of:
- Guaranteeing consummate customer satisfaction through superior products and excellent service;
- Maximising staff potential by providing an environment which encourages individual creativity and optimal productivity;
- Spending wisely while taking appropriate business risks in order to achieve rewarding results;
- Holding itself accountable to the highest ethical and regulatory standards;
- Adding value to the community by practicing corporate social responsibility;
- Leading the way in innovation and entrepreneurship.

With more than 1.5 billion dollars in assets under management, ABI is the leading financial conglomerate in Antigua and Barbuda.

The splendour of the natural world

KIM DERRICK

Hermit crab
Photo: Ann Granger

Blessed by year-round warm weather, the strong easterly Trade Winds, and a fairly well defined wet and dry season, Antigua and Barbuda sits on the north-easterly tip of the Caribbean archipelago. Antigua's average yearly temperature is 27⁰C, and during a normal year, the island receives about 45 inches of rainfall.

Antigua roughly divides into three distinct topographic regions: the volcanic south, the central plains and the north-eastern coral-limestone region. Barbuda is mainly characterised by sand dunes and limestone. Most of Antigua and Barbuda's land area is covered by dry savannah. On Antigua, the shrub-like mesquite and acacia dominate the landscape. Barbuda still possesses much of its original dry forest with white cedar predominating and large grassland areas of mostly Seymour grass.

Fringing coral reefs and rich mangrove areas surround much of both islands and provide important nurseries for many fish and shellfish species. Antigua and Barbuda has almost twice as many acres of mangrove as the rest of the English-speaking Lesser Antillean islands combined. Because they sit on the largest fishing bank in the Eastern Caribbean – the Barbuda Bank – Antigua and Barbuda is known for its exceptional sports fishing.

Mangrove areas provide excellent platforms for bird watching and learning about ecosystems. Barbuda's Codrington Lagoon is home to one of the world's most significant populations of magnificent frigate birds. Thousands of these majestic birds return to perform dramatic nesting rituals in the lagoon's isolated mangrove stands every year. The McKinnons Pond, on the

RIGHT
Nesting brown pelicans.
Photo: Eli Fuller

FACING PAGE
Morris Bay on the southern coast of Antigua.
Photo: Joseph Jones

CLOCKWISE FROM TOP

Male frigate bird
in mating ritual.
Photo: Ann Granger

The spiny lobster is found
throughout Caribbean waters.
Photo: David Vrancken

The brown pelican is a
regular visitor to the docks
and harbours.
Photo: Ann Granger

Southern stingray.
Photos: David Vrancken

The ground and tree lizards
are a common sight.
Photo: Ann Granger

The Caribbean experience is
not complete without the
ubiquitous sound of the tree
frog. This rarely-seen,
thumbnail-sized frog begins
its chirping at around sunset
or after a rain shower.
Photo: Martha Watkins-Gilkes

The green turtle is found
throughout the Caribbean.
Photo: David Vrancken

CLOCKWISE FROM TOP

The spectacular flamboyant tree in full bloom.
Photo: Joseph Jones

Green back heron.
Photo: Joseph Jones

Common octopus.
Photo: David Vrancken

The reefs provide a safe haven for many striking varieties of fish.
Photo: Martha Watkins-Gilkes

Beautiful and unusual flowers are everywhere.
Photo: Photogenesis

CLOCKWISE FROM TOP

Porkfish swimming among the many varieties of coral.
Photo: David Vrancken

The common moorhen.

One of the country's many butterfly species.

Pond lily.
Photos: Joseph Jones

The endangered West Indian whistling duck.
Photo: Mark Day

The unusual flying gurnard.
Photo: David Vrancken

TOP
A 'carpet' of pond
lilies just minutes
from V.C. Bird
International Airport.
Photo: Joseph Jones

RIGHT
Sheep making their
way to pasture in
Codrington, Barbuda.
Photo: Janet Jones

outskirts of St John's, transforms into a second home for numerous bird species between March and June. Species like the black necked stilt – which has the largest leg to body ratio of any bird after the flamingo – and white-cheeked pintail ducks, various herons, egrets, sandpipers and warblers can be spotted wading in the mudflats.

On the uninhabited North Sound islands glimpse relictual stands of the flora most closely resembling what Christopher Columbus would have encountered during his 15th century visits.

Because of their coral reefs, sea grass beds and mangrove, small fry literally jump out of the water when boats slice through the waves. This area is perhaps the jewel in the crown of Antigua's environmental assets. Here, the critically endangered Antigua racer snake, West Indian whistling duck, hawksbill and green turtles all make their home.

In the 17th century, fallow deer were introduced for hunting on the North Sound's Guiana Island and have survived until today due to the keen stewardship of the island. While boating there, if

The distinctive 'pink' beaches at Palmetto Point, on the south-western tip of Barbuda, derive their colour from the pink shell deposits that run along the coastline.

Photo: Joseph Jones

TOP
The rugged peninsula at Indian Town Point, on the east coast of Antigua, is home to Devil's Bridge. According to folklore, the site was so named because it was where runaway slaves used to go to commit suicide. Many would throw themselves off the 'bridge' and onto the treacherous rocks below during rough seas. Because of these mass suicides, it was said that, "the Devil had to be there."

LEFT
The 'Pillars of Hercules' are situated at the entrance to English Harbour. These spectacular rock formations are the result of millions of years of weather and sea erosion.

Photos: Joseph Jones

TOP
Colourful blooms adorn
many buildings.

RIGHT
Cattle taking the
afternoon shade.
Photos: Joseph Jones

you are quiet, you may glimpse these shy animals during early morning or late evening.

The North Sound islands are also home to innumerable seabirds. Brown pelicans, brown boobies, red-tailed tropic birds with their attractive tail streamers, American oystercatchers and several varieties of terns as well as the ever-present seagull, all compete for nesting sites on these tiny islands. If you're lucky you might see an osprey or two.

Although much of Antigua was deforested by the early 1700s to make way for sugar cane cultivation, many native plants still exist. Most of the island's evergreen deciduous forest remains on the southern peaks. A few southern valleys like the Wallings watershed, next to the scenic Fig Tree Drive, contain notable moist forest species. A nature hike along the Wallings' trails promises breathtaking coastal views and glimpses of lush flora such as a wild iris several orchid and bromeliad species, the majestic kapok or silk cotton, the curious, bearded ficus and the enormous fan-shaped leaf of the leather-coat tree, a relative of the sea side grape.

While hiking, listen for the shrill cries of the broad-winged hawk.

The black, lesser Antillean bullfinch, with his red throat, and the yellow-breasted banaquit which has black upper parts and sports a white stripe above the eye, are two of the islands' most common birds. Also often sighted are the zenaida dove, the ground dove and several species of hummingbird. Visitors may be surprised to see the introduced European house sparrow while in St John's.

When touring the island, you may glimpse the Indian mongoose scurrying for cover in roadside bushes. Since its 1870s introduction, the mongoose has reproduced to the detriment of many egg-laying species. In spite of this menace, ground and tree lizard populations abound on the islands, as do three types of gecko. The introduced marine toad has also become a pest species and can be seen throughout the islands. In contrast, two species of tree frog are rarely seen but are heard every evening performing one of nature's greatest symphonies.

A diversity of sporting activities, but cricket is still number one

FRANKLIN FRANCIS

Ever since the earliest days of British colonial rule, sport has been an integral part of Antigua and Barbuda's culture. In particular, cricket was part and parcel of the colonial enterprise and served as a means of expressing and implying the values of English society. Throughout the Caribbean – wherever the British were settled – cricket was the sport of choice.

By the early 20th century, several sporting clubs had emerged in Antigua although cricket, football and netball were the main recreational activities. These clubs reflected the social and racial divisions of the day with each representing and providing a rallying point for their respective communities. The British ruling classes also established lawn tennis clubs which were exclusive enclaves that barred all but the most 'connected' English folk.

However, it was in the field of cricket that local Antiguans were able to challenge the dominance of the colonialists. The country had been involved in various competitions between other Leeward Islands since 1913, competing for the Hesketh Bell Shield which had been donated by the then Governor of the Leeward Islands. At the time, the sport was dominated and controlled by the planter class but was eagerly followed and played by local Antiguans. Persistence paid off, and in 1940 Sydney Walling (now Sir Sydney Walling) became the first Black captain of an Antiguan team participating in the annual Leeward Islands tournament.

Other players emerged over the years gaining positions in the Antigua team and in the combined Leeward Islands team. Players such as Leo Gore, Eustace 'Tuss' Matthew and Malcolm Richards – father of the legendary Sir Vivian Richards – made names for themselves throughout the region. It was this rich tradition that fostered the long line of Antiguan players who graced the West Indies teams of the Seventies, Eighties and Nineties, beginning with Andy Roberts and Viv Richards in 1974 and culminating with Austin Richards Jr who earned a place in the West Indies squad that toured England in 2007. And the legacy is continuing

RIGHT
Since 1981, the Antigua Recreation Ground has been the home of cricket in Antigua and Barbuda.
Photo: Photogenesis

FACING PAGE
"Pappy" entertains supporters at the Sir Vivian Richards Cricket Stadium during the 2006 Cricket World Cup.
Photo: Joseph Jones

with Mali Richards – son of Sir Vivian – who currently holds the record for the highest individual score in the Leeward Islands tournament, and Devon Thomas who captained Leeward Islands in the 2007 West Indies Under-19 tournament.

Football has also enjoyed a long tradition in Antigua and Barbuda with the establishment of a football association in 1928. It was affiliated to the world governing body, FIFA, in 1970. The Antigua and Barbuda Football Association now boasts forty-two registered clubs and organises several annual competitions including a women's league. Although Antigua and Barbuda's national team currently languishes in

tenth position among Caribbean nations on the FIFA world ranking, several players have earned football scholarships to attend universities in the United States, and two players – Peter Byers and Gayson 'Bubbler' Gregory – are currently plying their trade in the semi-pro league in Trinidad and Tobago.

Track and Field and **Cycling** are sports that have also enjoyed some popularity in Antigua and Barbuda. Former Prime Minister, Lester Bird was one of the first to gain a medal in international competition. His long jump gold at the Pan Am Games in 1958 has since been followed by Heather Samuels (sprint medals at CAC Games and Pan Am games), Janil Williams

ABOVE
The Sir Vivian Richards Cricket Stadium was built with the assistance of the government of the People's Republic of China in time for the Cricket World Cup in 2007.

FAR RIGHT
The official hand-over ceremony was attended by representatives and dignitaries from both countries including Prime Minister Baldwin Spencer and China's Ambassador Wren.

RIGHT
Cricket legend Sir Vivian Richards was awarded 'National Hero' status on 1st November 2006. He retired in the 1990s as one of the most successful captains of the West Indies team. His contribution to world cricket was acknowledged with a knighthood which he received at the Antigua Recreation Ground in 1999.

Photos: Joseph Jones

(long distance double at the junior Pan Am games), James Grayman (Pan Am high jump bronze) and Brendan Christian (100-metre bronze and 200-metre gold at the 2007 Pan Am games in Brazil). Antigua and Barbuda has been represented at the Olympics since 1976 in various disciplines including Karl James's participation in sailing at the Sydney Olympics.

This highlights an area that should be prevalent in a small island nation – marine or aquatic sports. **Antigua Sailing Week** (now Stanford Antigua Sailing Week) has become one of the world's major yachting regattas and attracts over one hundred yachts and thousands of spectators every year. The event celebrated its 40th anniversary in 2007.

Boxing over the years has also enjoyed a following in Antigua and Barbuda and Maurice Hope – who held the World Middleweight title in the 1980s – still holds regular camps for young Antiguans and Barbudans, and organises participation in regional events. Bodybuilding has progressed over the years from the backyard gyms prevalent in the 1960s to more professional outfits. The sport's two leading protagonists – Steve Williams and Beverly Percival – were awarded the sportsman and sportswoman of the year titles, respectively, after gaining medals at CAC **bodybuilding** events in 2006.

While some hotels have golf courses, the main golfing activity takes place at the Cedar Valley Golf Club where growing numbers of

TOP
Following a lull in recent years, spectator numbers at the Cassada Gardens racetrack are beginning to rise.
Photo: Janet Jones

TOP
Soft ball cricket at the Rising
Sun Cricket Ground in St
John's would not be
complete without a picnic.
Photo: Joseph Jones

RIGHT
Growing numbers of
youngsters have been taking
an interest in golf.
Photo: Antigua and Barbuda Tourism
Department

youngsters have been taking an interest in this non-traditional sport.

Along with the influences of American culture, **basketball** has become increasingly popular in the last few decades. Several communities around the country have constructed flood-lit, outdoor court facilities while the government's Community Development Sports and Games Department hosts regular basketball, **netball** and **volleyball** competitions at their facility in the capital. Basketball has also provided an avenue for academic scholarships for young Antiguans and Barbudans.

Facilities are an important part of sporting development, and in recent years several urban and rural communities have begun upgrading their playing fields and sporting amenities. The new state-of-the-art Sir Vivian Richards Stadium, constructed as one of the host venues for the ICC Cricket World Cup 2007, has added new prestige to the sporting infrastructure. However, since 1981, the home of cricket in Antigua and Barbuda has been the Antigua Recreation Ground. It has seen many historic matches and has been the venue for a number of cricketing world records including the fastest Test century (Viv Richards, 1986); 375 runs not out, breaking Garfield Sobers' 1958 record of 365 runs not out (Brian Lara, 1994); and 400 runs not out (Brian Lara, 2004). The venue still retains its charm and appeal and has been one of the more popular cricket venues in the Caribbean.

Spectacular tournament to revitalise Caribbean cricket

The world's cricket community was bowled over by the inaugural Stanford 20/20 Tournament which took place in Antigua in the summer of 2006. Expectations were high, and the competition did not disappoint. Throughout the six-week contest, thousands of spectators were treated to electrifying and fun-filled matches at the Stanford Cricket Ground. Hundreds of thousands more across the Caribbean, along with millions around the world, tuned in to watch the spectacle. It was one of the most exiting sporting events to take place in the Caribbean in recent years, and even rivalled the Cricket World Cup which took place in the region in 2007.

The Stanford 20/20 Tournament is the brainchild of Sir Allen Stanford – Founder, Chairman and CEO of the Stanford Financial Group of Companies.

As well as providing an unmatched sporting event, the objective of the tournament is to revive cricket in the Caribbean. It aims to bring back the glory days of West Indies cricket and re-ignite interest in the game throughout the region. The programme will assist in the development of players and teams and will work towards establishing a professional cricket league.

The tournament has already left its mark on Antigua and Barbuda, but the Stanford 20/20 Professional League will ensure a legacy of

A resounding wicket for Antigua and Barbuda (right) and an enthusiastic appeal for 'out' (facing page) in the Stanford 20/20 Tournament.

Photos: Brooks La Touche Photography

cricket in the Caribbean that will endure for years to come. As the first of its kind in the Caribbean, the objective of the Stanford 20/20 Professional League is to encourage greater competition in the Stanford 20/20 Tournament and to develop new players for national teams and, ultimately, for the West Indies cricket team itself. As Sir Allen Stanford says, "The West Indies will benefit greatly from the calibre of cricket that comes out of this league."

In terms of cricket, Antigua and Barbuda already has a reputation for producing world-class and legendary cricketers such as Sir Vivian Richards, Andy Roberts, Richie Richardson and Curtly Ambrose. Their significant contribution to Caribbean cricket, and to the West Indies team, has been pivotal in the development of the game.

In the coming years, all eyes will be on Antigua and Barbuda for this showcase event. It will, in turn, further promote the country as an idyllic tourist destination. The Stanford 20/20 Tournament also provides a boost to the economy with increased visitor numbers and spin-off events.

More information about the Stanford 20/20 Tournament available from www.stanford2020.com.

Pictured against the backdrop of V.C. Bird International Airport, the Stanford Cricket Ground, above, is home to the Stanford 20/20 Cricket Tournament. The inaugural 2006 competition was won by Guyana. The victorious team is pictured, left, with Sir Allen Stanford, Founder, Chairman and CEO of the Stanford Financial Group of Companies, who presented them with a winner's cheque for US$1 million.

Photos: Joseph Jones

Celebrating the unsung influence of the women of the nation

MICKEL BRANN

The woman's story in patriarchal Antigua and Barbuda is more than a tale of the strong, yet silent, female behind the successful man. From Edith Richards (the first woman to seek elected office in 1956) to Dr Jacqui Quinn-Leandro (the first woman elected to Parliament in 2004) and all the success stories in between, women in the twin-island nation have good reason to feel proud.

While the representation might not be equal and the playing field far from level, young girls in modern-day Antigua and Barbuda certainly have role models to emulate.

In the field of politics, three women sit in the Upper House; Senator Gail Christian, Senator Joanne Massiah and President of the Senate, Hazelyn Francis. These women stand on the shoulders of the forerunners who were perceived, at best, as upstarts who were ahead of their time.

History will find special mention for Ruth Samuel, the first woman appointed to the Senate by the Progressive Labour Movement (PLM) administration; Senator Millicent Bailey, who was the first woman to serve at the pleasure of the Antigua Labour Party (ALP); and a sister from yesteryear, Bertha Higgins, who was appointed by the late Rt Hon. V.C. Bird Sr to the Federal Senate in 1958.

D. Gisele Isaac, who took the Speaker of the House baton from Dame Bridget Harris (the first woman to serve in that capacity), is executive secretary at the Board of Education. Kathleen Forde is the boss at Central Marketing Corporation (CMC); Dr Ermina Osoba is the chairwoman of the Board of Education; Valerie Hodge has responsibility for the National Parks Foundation; and Dr Linda Lovell-Roberts is the government's Acting Chief Medical Officer. Of the eighteen permanent secretaries, twelve are women: Vincere Bachelor, Governor-General's Office; Barbara Belle, Ministry of Justice and Legal Affairs; Cecily Phillip, Ministry of Information and Broadcasting; Venessa Matthews, Ministry of Works and Transportation; Venessa Nicholas, Ministry of

Labour and Public Affairs; Ruthlyn Hector, Establishment Department; Bernadette George, Prime Minister's Office; Sharon Zane Peters, Ministry of Tourism; Elaine Carter, Ministry of Civil Aviation, Culture and Environment; Agatha Warrington, Ministry of Sport and Youth Affairs; Brenda Cornelius, Attorney-General and Legal Affairs; and Doleen Lee, Ministry of Finance and Economy.

In 2007, Louise Lake-Tack became the country's first woman Governor-General. She joins the impressive ranks of women who occupy leading positions in Antigua and Barbuda which include Commissioner of Police, Delano Christopher; Director of Audit, Veronica Browne; the Ombudsman, J.M. Eusalyn Lewis; Senior Analyst in the Establishment Department, Stacey Gregg; and the Chief Protocol Officer, Cisley Solomon.

In business, the lore accords a handsome helping of reverence to the memory of the late Sissy Nathan, a landowner and moneylender from the 1940s. "She was powerful, a person to be reckoned with," mused historian Selvyn Walter who, as a young boy, read for the ageing Nathan. Her industriousness has helped pave the way for women like Eileen Murraine, the first woman in the Eastern Caribbean to be appointed General Manager within the Royal Bank of Canada.

The woman's story in Antigua and Barbuda would not be complete without paying homage to the merchants (who traded mostly in fabric) including Mary John, Gisele Michael and the maverick, Edris Silston, who was among the first to retail ready-made clothes.

The art sorority celebrates Higgins as the mother of the movement in Antigua and Barbuda. In the 1940s, before steelband took its pride of place, she invited members of the Hell's Gate Steel Orchestra into her living room and taught them to read and write music. Tribute must also be paid to another first lady; Director of Culture, Heather Doram, who is an artist, actress, costume designer and the creator of the national dress. And we must not forget the female calypsonians, who have razed the boys' playground in recent years, not least among them the diminutive, twice-crowned monarch, Lena "Queen Ivena" Philip. Or the women

TOP
Governor-General Louise Lake-Tack, left, with Commissioner of Police Delano Christopher during the Governor-General's swearing-in ceremony.

LEFT
During his visit to Antigua and Barbuda in 2006, HRH Prince Edward visited the Sunshine Home for Girls. The orphanage plays a vital role in looking after young girls throughout their formative years.
Photos: Joseph Jones

In 2004, Dr Jacqui Quinn-Leandro became the first woman to be elected to Parliament, and in 2007, she became the first women to be acting Prime Minister.
Photo: Joseph Martin

Former model turned restaurateur, Yvonne "Candy" Pilgrim has run the Candy Lane beach bar and restaurant since 1976. Located near the historic Fort James, the venue is popular with locals and tourists alike.

Increasing numbers of women are embarking on entrepreneurial activities including the production of arts and crafts, clothing and beauty products. Events such as the Independence Craft Expo are ideal showcases for their businesses.
Photo: Joseph Jones

Senator Joanne Massiah is Minister Responsible for Marine Affairs and Food Production.
Photo: Joseph Martin

responsible for putting the country on the literary and film industry map, like Jamaica Kincaid, Joanne Hillhouse and the present Speaker of the House, who penned Antigua's first two feature-length movies, *The Sweetest Mango* and *No Seed*.

In the field of education, women are at the forefront, dating back to the era of the Spring Gardens Moravian Teachers Training College, whose principals aimed to empower women in this regard. Avis Athill, Agatha Goodwin, Mary Pigott, Nellie Robinson and Gwen Tonge, who brought respectability to home economics, are some of the educators lifted onto pedestals. And it is difficult to ignore the fact that the latest statistics show that girls are outperforming boys in the classroom.

Sportswomen, too, have hoisted Antigua and Barbuda's flag high in the international arena, namely middle and long-distance runner, Janill Williams who struck gold at the Pan American Junior Games in 2001, and Desiree Francis who, in 2000, was selected to play (albeit for one season) in the WNBA for the New York Liberty.

"Women have been the unheralded, unsung and unrecognised leaders who have helped to shape the society," Walter said. This is about much more than cigarettes and smoke, but the American slogan, "You've come a long way, baby" rings true.

From colonial oppression to independent nation

EDWARD T. HENRY

Antigua and Barbuda was colonised specifically as a mercantile resource for the production of sugar. No serious attempts at colonisation took place until 1632 when a party of Englishmen, under the leadership of Edward Warner, set out from nearby St Kitts and landed on the southern side of Antigua and claimed it for the English Crown. They established a tenuous settlement where they lived in a state of perpetual crisis. They were under attack from the Caribs and were caught up in the wars between the English, French and Dutch as well as in the feuds of the Restoration.

The early settlers cultivated cash crops such as tobacco, indigo, cotton and ginger for export and subsistence crops for themselves. In succeeding years, sugar came into prominence. Its production shaped Antigua's landscape to this day when vast areas of rainforest were cleared to make way for sugarcane fields. During the seventeenth century, Antigua was one of the most heavily wooded islands in the Eastern Caribbean and its trees were felled to supply timber and spares for ships. Lignum vitae and other useful plants – which are now largely extinct - then flourished. The island boasted two small rivers, one at Carlisle and the other at Blubber Valley.

In 1674, a dramatic change in the island's economy took place when the first large-scale sugar plantation was established by Sir Christopher Codrington who came from Barbados. He named his estate Betty's Hope after his daughter. His success encouraged others to turn to sugar production. More than 150 sugar mills dotted the countryside, many of which are still standing today. The early planters christened many of their large estates with names that are familiar in Antigua today: Byam, Duers, Gunthorpes, Lucas, Parry, Vernon, Cochran and Winthorpe.

In 1710, Governor Park was killed in a stand off between his own militia and the planters of the day. In 1728, there was a minor slave uprising and in 1736, a major slave rebellion was alleged to have been uncovered. The three

RIGHT & FACING PAGE
Nineteenth century impressions of African slaves cutting cane on an Antiguan sugar estate and the Gracehill Estate.

ring-leaders, Court, Tomboy and Hercules, were 'broken' on the wheel and some eighty others brutally executed.

In 1834, slavery in Antigua and Barbuda was abolished but slaves were not 'free' in the real sense of the word; and Antiguans were still scarred from the colonial experience. Emancipation further perpetuated the hierarchy of colour and race that the British had established at the beginning of the colonial period. Stringent Acts were passed to ensure that the planters had a constant supply of labour.

The Assembly voted in June 1846 to import Portuguese workers from Madeira and the Cape Verde Islands. About 2000 arrived between 1847 and 1856, mostly from Madeira. They were brought to the island to replace the workers who left the sugar estates in order to gain recruitment in the West India army. In the early 1900s, ethnic diversity increased with the arrival of itinerant traders or 'peddlers' who came from Lebanon.

When, in early 1918, the planters decided to change the method by which cane was paid for at the factory, the result was the riot of 9 March 1918. During the disturbances, many people were killed or injured, but the planters' decision on cane payment was reversed.

The founding of the Antigua Trades and Labour Union on the instigation of Sir Walter Citrine, a member of the Moyne Commission that visited the West Indies in 1938/9, marked a significant step in the development of labour relations between the planters of the day and the labourers. Most of the workers lost no time in becoming members of the trade union and, for the first time in over one hundred years, workers could be assured that their rights were protected. Among other things, the Antigua Trades and Labour Union, with its President Reginald Stevens, initiated bargaining processes with the planters and under the dynamic leadership of Vere Cornwall Bird, who succeeded him, made even greater strides in having the rights of the workers respected. The struggle for the recognition of the rights of the workers was a long and bitter one.

The opening of US military bases in 1941 placed the United States at the centre of Antigua's economic and social life but sugar remained the dominant, although declining, sector of the economy throughout the 1940s and 1950s.

TOP
The Martello Tower is located near River Beach in the south of Barbuda. Built onto a pre-existing fort in the early 19th century, this defensive tower was used to defend the south-western coast of the island. It housed a small garrison of soldiers and at least three cannons.
Photo: Joseph Jones

LEFT
Nineteenth century impression of slave labourers loading barrels of sugar into rowing boats for transfer to ships anchored in Willoughby Bay.

The Antigua Labour Party (ALP), with its trade union base, fought and won all subsequent elections, save one when the Progressive Labour Movement (PLM) won in 1971 and George Walter became Premier. But the ALP was again returned to power in 1976. Under the Bird administration, Antigua achieved independence in association with Great Britain in 1967, and full independence in 1981. In March 2004, the Antigua Labour Party was defeated at the polls for only the second time in its history. The United Progressive Party (UPP), under the leadership of Baldwin Spencer, won the elections and formed the Government.

With a population of around 1500 people, Barbuda is a relatively flat island of limestone formation lying approximately thirty miles north of Antigua. Its highest point is a mere 128 feet

in an area known as The Highlands. The island boasts one of the finest beaches in the Caribbean which is located at Coco Point.

Barbuda has had a long history of dependence, first as a private leasehold of the Codrington family (1685-1870), then as a Crown colony and later as a dependency of Antigua. For many years, the political relationship between Antigua and Barbuda has been an uneasy one but with the recent success of the United Progressive Party at the polls, bold steps have been taken to improve this situation and a member of the Barbuda Council (which was formed in 1977) now sits as a member of the Cabinet of Antigua and Barbuda.

When Barbuda became a part of the new state of Antigua and Barbuda in 1981, its natural endowments were disrupted. It was clear that its small-scale productive economy that, in the previous century, relied on the salvage of ship wrecks, fishing, hunting and farming, could not continue to support the needs of a growing population. Many people emigrated but kept in touch with the homeland, making remittances to their families from time to time.

Over the past three decades, its natural resources, particularly its beaches, have become vulnerable to commercial exploitation. Sadly, Barbuda has benefited fractionally from the vast revenues drawn from the sand mining industry over the years and its environment is now in danger of being seriously impaired.

Preserving the nation's treasures

REG MURPHY

English Harbour, in the Parish of St Paul, has a long and colourful history. It was first settled approximately 4000 years ago by Archaic Age fisher/forager peoples. They were a nomadic, marine-oriented culture that utilised the marine and terrestrial resources of the area. These peoples are believed to have originated from South America, migrating north through the islands in small groups. Evidence of their occupation has been found by archaeologists on the seafront near to Clarence House, and the mangrove flats near to Cobbs Cross.

During the middle of the first millennium BC, they were displaced by pottery-making, Arawak people from the lower Orinoco region of South America. The Arawaks introduced many of the edible and useful plants to Antigua that are still used today. These include cotton, tobacco, papaya, guava, pineapple, cassava and corn. They established large settlements at Indian Creek, Mamora Bay, Freeman's Bay, Rendezvous Bay to name a few. The Arawaks were to occupy Antigua until the arrival of the European explorers in 1493. By the time of English settlement in 1632, the native peoples - dubbed 'Caribs' by the Europeans - had abandoned Antigua and Barbuda. However, the rich marine resources of the island was essential to their survival and resistance against the English colonists continued sporadically for another fifty years.

Although it is debatable exactly which European was the first to settle in Antigua, credit is generally attributed to Edward Warner for his successful colonisation of the island. Members of the Warner family themselves in the Piccadilly area, and the tombs in their private cemetery, although badly vandalised, can still be seen today. Archaeological investigations are currently in progress at this site to gain insights into the life and times of this little-known period of Antigua's history - the early years before sugar and slavery.

During these early years, Falmouth was established as a place of commerce and settlement and English Harbour as a safe harbour for shelter and repair of ships. Further development saw the establishment of the British Naval facilities - the Antigua Dockyard, now called the Nelson's Dockyard – followed by the numerous army barracks built on Shirley Heights. Throughout this period, everything was built using the labour of African slaves.

With political recognition of the importance and values of the south-eastern coast of Antigua, the Nelson's Dockyard National Park was established in 1984. The National Parks Authority (NPA) was established by Act of Parliament to manage, conserve, protect and develop the rich cultural, historical, archaeological and natural resources of the area. Covering approximately eleven square miles (about ten percent of Antigua), the park begins at Mamora Bay and ends at Carlisle Bay. The demarcation line follows the ridges of the coastal highlands or watershed. After an initial lengthy public consultation process, the area was zoned, with each area designated for specific types of development. These include tourism, residential community, conservation and natural habitat zones. This policy serves to guide and ensure the sustainable development of the area and stands as a successful model that should be applied to the rest of the island.

To implement its mandate, the National Parks generates revenue through user fees - admission, rental of restored buildings, and management of its resources such as the marina and hotel. The dockyard is viewed as a continuing cultural landscape and strives to maintain a balance of historical authenticity within a 21st century technological environment.

One of its strongest yet least-known sectors of the National Park is its research and archaeology program. The Dockyard Museum and Field Research Centre host annual field schools with the University of Calgary and many interns, graduates and researchers visit annually to work under the supervision of the museum and archaeology director. This joint program continues to add new and tangible insights into the history and material culture of the islands and the surrounding areas.

Nelson's Dockyard National Park is the gem of St Paul's and is one of the leading heritage tourism attractions in the Eastern Caribbean. The beautiful landscapes and the rich history and seafaring culture, contribute significantly to the economy of Antigua and Barbuda.

Nelson's Dockyard

English Harbour is one of the safest anchorages in the Caribbean. With its natural deep water, flanked by protective hills rising to over 450 feet, it was developed by the British Navy as a dockyard in the middle of the 18th century. Later named Nelson's Dockyard in honour of its most famous resident, Britain's Admiral Horatio Nelson, the dockyard stands in tribute to the 'age of sail'. As one of the finest remaining Georgian naval facilities of its day, the dockyard continues to function as a facility dedicated to the service and accommodation of seafarers and their vessels. It is the historical core of the National Parks of Antigua and Barbuda, a protected area and the premiere heritage tourism destination in Antigua.

The historical structures and naval facilities have been recently restored and upgraded to the best international standards, and with its many fine restaurants, boutiques, museums, nature trails and handicrafts, Nelson's Dockyard has become a unique, world class heritage site.

TOP
Sea wall reconstruction and bullet shells and cannon balls excavated in 2002.
Photos: Reg Murphy

The legacy of Admiral Nelson

EDWARD T. HENRY

Situated in the south-east of Antigua, Nelson's Dockyard, along with the surrounding Shirley Heights and Monks Hill, comprise the most scenic and historically attractive part of the island. Named after England's naval hero, Admiral Horatio Nelson, the dockyard has become one of the most popular sites in Antigua for tourists and yachtsmen alike.

Construction of the dockyard was initiated in 1725 by Captain Arthur Delgarno of HMS Southsea Castle, who reported to the Royal Navy that "English Harbour might be made a very proper place for careening and refitting, and so save HMS ships the trouble of going to northern colonies for that purpose". His report was accepted and supported by the Antigua Legislature which purchased twenty acres of land and presented them to the Admiralty.

Construction of a careening wharf began on the eastern side of the harbour and a fort was built to replace the small battery that guarded the entrance. Within three years the first dockyard, then called St Helena, was in use. Further development of the site continued throughout most of the 18th century.

English Harbour gained prominence after Britain lost the American colonies following the American Revolution (1775-1783), with activity at the harbour reaching a peak during the Napoleonic Wars (1800-1815).

At more than 275 years old, the harbour has become a thriving yacht basin which has undergone careful renovations and development to maintain and enhance its historic value. Every year, the dockyard plays host to sailing regattas and boat shows which have gained international recognition.

ABOVE RIGHT
Admiral Nelson's bedchamber has been preserved in the building which is now the Dockyard Museum.
Photo: J Martin / Photogenesis

RIGHT
Built in 1798, the Copper and Lumber Store at Nelson's Dockyard is now a hotel bearing the same name.
Photo: Joseph Jones

Leaders of the nation since 1967

IVOR FORD

SIR VERE CORNWALL BIRD, ON, KNH
Premier, 1967 – 1971 & 1976 – 1981
Prime Minister, 1981 – 1994

Sir Vere Cornwall Bird was Antigua and Barbuda's first Prime Minister. He was born on 9 December 1909 at New Street, on the southern fringes of the capital, St John's. He was the fourth of five children of Barbara Edghill and Theophilus 'Thophy' Bird. The young Vere Bird was educated at the St John's Boys' School.

He joined the Salvation Army and was sent to Jamaica for training. This opportunity offered him the chance to visit several islands in the Caribbean, where he was able to witness the deplorable living conditions in which the people were compelled to live.

In 1939, V.C. Bird was one of a number of Antiguans and Barbudans who were privileged to attend a meeting convened at the Anglican Cathedral School Room on Long Street. This meeting was at the instigation of Sir Walter Citrine, a member of the Royal Commission that was sent to the region to investigate the root causes of riots that engulfed the entire region in the late 1930s. The Commission was headed by Lord Moyne, a respected member of the House of Lords in the British Parliament.

On 16 January 1939, the momentous decision was taken to form a trade union in Antigua and Barbuda and, shortly thereafter, the Antigua Trades & Labour Union (AT&LU) was born. However, it was not until 3 March 1940 that the union was officially recognised under the Trades Union Act. The first President of the new union was Reginald St Clair Stevens, a businessman in St John's. In 1942, V.C. Bird became the second President of the AT&LU. Soon after his ascension to the presidency of the AT&LU, a decision was taken by the union that V.C. Bird should seek election to the Legislative Council. This was successfully achieved in 1946.

Acknowledged as the 'Father of the Nation', Vere Cornwall Bird served twice as Premier and was Prime Minister for thirteen years.

In January 1960, Vere Cornwall Bird was appointed the first Chief Minister of Antigua and Barbuda. This new responsibility was a result of constitutional improvement for the territory. As Chief Minister, V.C. Bird was in command of the political structure in Antigua and Barbuda. From the powerful position of leadership and influence of the work force and the machinery of Government, he became even more powerful, both on the labour front and at the legislative level.

In 1962, following the dissolution of the Federation of the West Indies, V.C. Bird extended a formal invitation to the leaders of the Windward and Leeward Islands and Barbados to join him in Antigua in search of a solution to the problems created by the withdrawal of both Trinidad and Tobago and Jamaica from the Federation. The feeling at the time was that the remaining eight nations should form another federation without the involvement of the larger territories. This group was to be known as 'The Little Eight'.

On 27 February 1967, another constitutional improvement was instituted when Antigua and Barbuda assumed a new status of Independence in Association with Great Britain. This unique model of parliamentary democracy was known as 'Associated Statehood'. It meant that the government of Antigua and Barbuda was responsible for all internal national matters while London retained responsibility for external affairs and defence.

However, the new Premier's greatest political challenge was the serious fracture of the AT&LU which caused a parting of the ways between V.C. Bird and one of his chief lieutenants, George H. Walter, the then dismissed General-Secretary of the AT&LU. The split brought into existence an opposition force of such magnitude that it precipitated a hasty retreat from political office of the hitherto seemingly invincible political arm of the AT&LU, the Antigua Labour Party (ALP).

The turbulent period between 1967 and 1976 was a traumatic time for the ALP and its companion organisation, the AT&LU. In 1971, the ALP lost the General Elections and was only able to retain four of the seventeen seats in Parliament. The leadership of V.C. Bird was tested because of the overwhelming support of the newly-established Progressive Labour Movement (PLM) which was led by George H. Walter. However, V.C. Bird triumphed in 1976 when he was handed the baton of power, once again, by the electorate.

Five years later, and one year into his successive election victory at the polls, Antigua and Barbuda gained independence from Britain and Vere Cornwall Bird received the Instruments of Independence from Britain's Princess Margaret on Sunday, 1 November 1981.

And so, after holding the position of Prime Minister of Antigua and Barbuda for twelve years, Vere Cornwall Bird voluntarily gave up the seat of political power. Six years later, the 'Father of the Nation' died on Monday, 28 June 1999. He was the recipient of the country's highest national award, 'National Hero'. He was also one of the first CARICOM citizens to be awarded the Order of Caricom.

Vere Cornwall Bird, the nation's first Prime Minister, died at the age of 89 having served his native Antigua and Barbuda for more than 54 years.

SIR GEORGE HERBERT WALTER, KGCN
Premier, 1971 – 1976

Born on 8 September 1928, into one of Antigua and Barbuda's most famous families, Sir George Herbert Walter is the second of ten children born to Norris and Marietta Walter who lived at the heart of the Capital, St John's.

At seventeen years old, he graduated from the prestigious Antigua Grammar School, and was then invited by his father to manage the family farm at Rendezvous Bay, several miles outside St John's. The following decade of managerial experience was to serve him well during his trade union and political careers.

In 1958, Sir George was chosen to manage and edit the Antigua Trades & Labour Union's (AT&LU) financially-struggling newspaper, *The Workers' Voice*. Within six months, however, the publication was operating at a profit under its young editor and enterprising manager. Two years later, on 4 January 1960, George H. Walter was elected as General Secretary of the AT&LU, replacing Lionel Hurst, who was promoted to the ministerial post of Minister of Labour in a newly-constituted V.C. Bird Government.

After his selection as AT&LU 'Man of the Year' in 1967, he was dismissed as General-Secretary four days later. This executive decision resulted in a serious fracture to the AT&LU that irrevocably altered the industrial and political landscape of Antigua and Barbuda. In 1968, social unrest led to the formation of a new political party – the Progressive Labour Movement (PLM).

Riding on the crest of a popular wave of support, the PLM defeated the Antigua Labour Party (ALP) in the 1971 General Elections, and George H. Walter was sworn in as the nation's second Premier on Friday, 12 February 1971. Five years later, his party lost the 1976 elections.

His services were acknowledged in the special Millennium Honours List of 2000, with one of the nation's highest awards – the Knight Grand Cross of the Nation (KGCN).

SIR WILFRED JACOBS, GCMG, KCVO, QC, OBE
Governor-General, 1981 – 1993

Sir Wilfred Ebenezer Jacobs was born in Grenada on 19 October 1919. His parents were William Henry Jacobs of Cedar Grove, Antigua, and Henrietta Dubois of Grenada. He was the first and only Associated Statehood Governor of Antigua and Barbuda, the first Governor-General of Antigua and Barbuda, and a former Attorney-General and Puisne Judge of Barbados.

Sir Wilfred was educated at the Anglican Boys' School of Grenada, where his father was Headmaster, and then went on to the Grenada Grammar School for his secondary education.

His decision to pursue a vocation in the legal profession was hindered by the outbreak of the Second World War, which meant that his early legal courses were taken in Grenada. He later travelled to England to do his Bar Finals before being called to the Bar. Sir Wilfred's progress in the legal profession was outstanding. He served in the Federation of the West Indies until its dissolution in 1962. Shortly thereafter,

Sir James Carlisle served as Governor-General for fourteen years until 2007.

he was appointed as Attorney-General of Barbados and was later promoted to the Bench as a Resident Puisne Judge.

In 1967, Sir Wilfred was invited to be the first Governor of the Associated State of Antigua and Barbuda. He served in this post for just over fourteen years until – upon the attainment of full independence in 1981 – he was sworn in as the nation's first Governor-General. After twelve years as Governor-General, Sir Wilfred officially retired from active public service in 1993. He died on 11 July 1995.

SIR JAMES CARLISLE, GCMG, KGN, GCQS, BDS
Governor-General, 1993 – 2007

Sir James Beethoven Carlisle was born in the village of Bolans on the 5 August 1937. He received his early education at the Bolans Public School. On successful completion of the Seventh Standard Examination, he was appointed as a pupil teacher. Anxious to develop himself further he emigrated to England in 1960.

At first, he worked and lived in London and attended evening classes at the Workingmen's College in St Pancras and the Northwestern Polytechnic in Kentish Town. Finding it difficult to work and also study he decided to join the Royal Air Force in 1961 so that he could take advantage of the educational opportunities being offered. While in the RAF he served in the Medical Branch and was posted to various parts of the United Kingdom.

In 1963, he was chosen to attend a Decompression Chamber Operating Course at the Royal Aircraft Establishment at Farnborough. Having successfully completed

LEFT
Sir Wilfred Jacobs was sworn in as Governor-General when the nation achieved full independence in 1981.

the course he was posted to Singapore where he was the sole decompression chamber operator in the Far East Air Force (FEAF). While serving in Singapore, Sir James was given permission to attend the University of Singapore where he pursued a non-graduating science course.

He was introduced to dentistry by an RAF dental officer and was so fascinated with the profession that he decided to become a dentist. After he was demobbed in 1966 he spent one year studying the required science subjects at the Northampton College of Technology in order to gain entrance to a British university. In 1967, he was admitted to the University of Dundee in Scotland where he studied dentistry. After graduation he worked as a dental surgeon in Scotland, Wales and England and returned to Antigua in 1979.

Sir James specialised in laser dentistry in Orlando, Florida in 1991 and became a member of the American Academy of Laser Dentistry and the International Association of Laser Dentistry. He was also a member of the British Dental Association and the Antigua and Barbuda Dental Association. In Antigua he established a successful dental practice and was responsible for initiating a fluoride program for school children. He also developed a free dental care program for the elderly. Sir James also gave volunteer service at the Baptist Dental Clinic and the Catholic Dental Clinic.

Despite his busy schedule he still found time for community service. He served as Chairman of the Tabitha Senior Citizens Home. In addition, he served as the Second Chairman of the National Parks Authority and played an important part in the establishment of the Nelson's Dockyard National Park.

On 10 June 1993, Sir James was sworn in as the second Governor-General of Antigua and Barbuda. In this capacity he contributed to regional integration by initiating the First Caricom Heads of State Conference in 1994. This conference is now an annual event. It provides the only forum for the interaction of the region's heads of state.

In November 1993, Sir James was awarded the Knight Grand Cross of the Most Distinguished Order of St Michael and St George (GCMG). Since then, he has been the recipient of several awards and honorary degrees including the Knight Grand Cross of the Order of Sheba (GCQS), the Knight Grand

Collar of the Most Distinguished Order of the Nation (KGN), and the Knight of Justice in the Most Venerable Order of St. John (KStJ). He was awarded an honorary degree of Doctor of Laws (LLD) by Andrews University in 1996 and an Honorary Fellowship in Dental Surgery by the Royal College of Surgeons of Edinburgh in 1995.

On 17 July 2007, Sir James Carlisle retired from the office of Governor-General. During his term he served as Patron of the Government House Restoration Trust (Founder), the Clarence House Restoration Trust (Founder), the Scouts Association, the Red Cross, Rotary Club, the Jaycees, the Boys' Brigade, Antigua and Barbuda Single Parents Association (Founder), the Antigua and Barbuda Beautification Commission (Founder) and many other national organisations.

LESTER BIRD
Prime Minister, 1994 – 2004

Lester Bryant Bird was born in the United States on 21 February 1938 and is the third child of the late Sir Vere Cornwall Bird Sr and Lady Lydia Bryant. Like most of his contemporaries, the son of one of Antigua and Barbuda's most influential leaders attended the Antigua Grammar School where he excelled in sports and athletics.

As a young and physically fit athlete, he represented Antigua and Barbuda and his alma mater nationally, regionally and internationally. In cricket, he was one of the region's most feared fast bowlers. It was the general view at the time that he should have represented the West Indies at Test match level. There were also those knowledgeable sporting experts who felt that he was excellent Olympic material who should have gone further.

His foray into politics followed his athletic achievements, beginning in 1971 when he was appointed leader of the opposition Antigua Labour Party (ALP) in the Senate of Antigua and Barbuda after unsuccessfully contesting the Barbuda seat against Claude E. Francis of the Progressive Labour Movement (PLM). However, in 1976, he was elected to Parliament and was appointed Deputy Premier to his father V.C. Bird Sr. He also served as Minister of Economic Development, Tourism and Foreign Affairs from where he learned the principles of government administration from his experienced father.

On 10 March 1994, Lester Bryant Bird assumed the office of Prime Minister of Antigua and Barbuda after successfully contesting his first general elections as political leader of the ALP. Exactly one decade after his stewardship as Prime Minister, Lester Bird was replaced by Winston Baldwin Spencer of the United Progressive Party (UPP).

In addition to his interest in politics and sports, Lester Bird has revealed another of his latent talents as a poet. In April 2003, he released a book of many of his speeches (*Antigua Vision: Caribbean Reality*) and an anthology of his poetry (*A Bird's Eye View*). The former Prime Minister is also a British-trained lawyer.

WINSTON BALDWIN SPENCER
Prime Minister, 2004 –

Winston Baldwin Spencer, the fourth child of Joyce Martin and Frederick Spencer, was born on 8 October 1948 in the suburbs of Antigua's capital, St John's. This quiet, respectful and affable man from Green Bay/Grays Farm (affectionately known locally as 'The Ghetto' or 'The Mud') received his early education at the Green Bay Government School and later obtained a scholarship to the Princess Margaret Secondary School. This was the first Government school in Antigua and Barbuda to offer free secondary education to the children of low income families.

During his formative years, he was active in the Antigua Trades & Labour Union (AT&LU). He was a member of the Young Juvenile Section of the Union and later, leader of the Youth

Baldwin Spencer is the nation's third Prime Minister.

Section of the AT&LU in Green Bay/Grays Farm. Baldwin Spencer's leadership skills were identified by the then President of the AT&LU, the late Sir Vere Cornwall Bird Sr who lobbied the Political Committee of the Union to send young Spencer for training in trade unionism and politics. He excelled at these subjects, thus fortifying his industrial and political future.

The rupture of the AT&LU and subsequent formation of its splinter rival union, the Antigua Workers' Union (AWU) on 31 May 1967, reflected a shrewdness in Baldwin Spencer which has influenced all his thoughts and actions to this day. Upon returning home from training in industrial relations at Ruskin College, Oxford in the UK, the young union field officer dutifully reported to the AT&LU. But subsequent events placed him firmly in the camp of the opposition movement.

Although not prominent in the front line of politics at the time, the young Baldwin Spencer was an important leader of the youth arm of the Progressive Labour Movement (PLM), the political affiliate of the AWU.

In 1989, Baldwin Spencer contested and won the St John's Rural West Parliamentary seat in the general elections. This was against Donald 'DC' Christian, who had occupied the seat since 1976.

In Parliament, Spencer skilfully weathered that first five years of challenges with great dexterity and determination. During this baptism of fire, he found an ally in Hilbourne Frank, the Independent Member for Barbuda. At the birth of the United Progressive Party (UPP) in 1992, Baldwin Spencer was elevated to the Leader's seat. The 1994 general elections pitched the UPP's Baldwin Spencer against the Antigua Labour Party's (ALP) James 'Tanny' Rose. He was again victorious, garnering 1,608 votes against Rose's 842.

And so, after fifteen years' experience in the Antigua and Barbuda Parliament, Winston Baldwin Spencer, on Wednesday, 24 March 2004, was sworn in by Governor-General, Sir James B. Carlisle as the nation's third Prime Minister.

LOUISE LAKE-TACK
Governor-General, 2007 –

When Louise Agnetha Lake-Tack became Governor-General of Antigua and Barbuda in July 2007, she became the first ever women to hold the position.

Born on 26 July 1944 at Long Lane Estate in the Parish of St Phillip's, she was educated at the Freetown Government School before attending the Antigua Girls High School in St John's.

After graduation, she emigrated to the United Kingdom where she pursued studies in nursing at the Charring Cross Hospital. She obtained her State Registered Nurse (SRN) qualification and gained employment at the National Heart Hospital and the Harley Street Clinic. After a number of years, Louise gave up her nursing career to take care of her family.

When her children reached adulthood, Louise Lake-Tack attended a number of educational institutions including City of Westminster College, Thames Valley University, the Open University, Holborn Law School and the Council of Legal Education to study for the bar. She successfully achieved a BA (Hons) and an LLB (Hons).

Mrs Lake-Tack has served as a magistrate since 1995 at both Marylebone and Horseferry Magistrate Courts in London. She also sat at Pocock Street Crown Court and Middlesex Crown Court to hear appeals from the lower courts.

A devout member of the Anglican Church, Mrs Lake-Tack studied for one year to become a Christian Counsellor at her local church, All Souls, Langham Place, London. She also worked as a volunteer in the All Souls Christian bookshop for several years.

RIGHT
Louise Lake-Tack became Antigua and Barbuda's first woman Governor-General.

Mrs Lake-Tack is a former member of the Anti-Apartheid Movement and helped to raise funds for the educational arm of that movement. She has been a member of the Antigua and Barbuda National Association (London) for the past twenty-four years, and has sat on the church committee of that group which was instrumental in arranging the annual Antigua and Barbuda Independence Church Service in London.

As a member of the Antigua and Barbuda National Association (London), she has helped to raise funds for hurricane victims in Antigua and Barbuda as well as for the St Phillip's Anglican Church which was devastated by hurricane Luis in 1995. At the rededication service of the St Phillip's Anglican Church in 1997, Mrs Lake-Tack accepted an award from Arch Bishop, Dr Orland Lindsay and Reverend Stapleton on behalf of the Antigua and Barbuda National Association (London) for their contribution towards the restoration of the church.

Mrs Lake-Tack has been a member of the British Red Cross Society since her teenage years in Antigua and Barbuda and has been awarded for her fundraising efforts. She personally provides funding for the private education of a number of children in Antigua and Barbuda.

A government built on freedom, fairness and electoral reform

BRUCE GOODWIN

It can be said that the modern political history of Antigua and Barbuda began in 1951, the year universal adult suffrage was granted the territory by the British colonial overlords. Prior to then, the right to vote in elections was limited to individuals who satisfied certain requirements of property ownership and income. Such requirements excluded the vast majority of Antiguans and Barbudans from participation in the political affairs of their country, since, at that time, the people of this country, for the most part, existed in a state of the most abject poverty and neglect.

While the granting of universal adult suffrage in 1951 reflected a new policy of the British government towards its colonies in the West Indies generally, the vehicle of struggle that the Antiguan and Barbudan people had used to advance their cause was the Antigua Trades and Labour Union (AT&LU), founded in 1939 and led by Vere Cornwall Bird Sr since 1941. Thus, the first really free general elections in the history of Antigua and Barbuda were those of 1951, which resulted in the formation of the first Labour Party government, with Vere Bird Sr as Chief Minister and a Cabinet comprising four of his elected colleagues; Messrs E.H. Lake, E.E. Williams, Machesney George and L. Hurst.

This first labour government is remembered for its integrity, openness and transparency. It inspired great confidence in the people of the country, who were motivated to work hard to redress the disadvantages and absence of opportunity that characterised the post-slavery colonial era that had begun with the abolition of slavery in 1834 and lasted until 1951.

Thus, the first decade of self-government was characterised by a number of highly successful initiatives in the areas of agricultural and industrial development. The Peasant Development Office (PDO), a department of the Ministry of Agriculture, pioneered a new system of land tenure and agricultural development, leading to the empowerment of a new class of independent small farmers that performed in an exemplary manner in the production of food crops, cotton, sugar cane, and small livestock. In these early years, the agricultural production of this sector soared, enabling the people to achieve a good measure of food security and to earn new levels of income that was used to better their social conditions of housing, health care, and education for their children.

Moreover, this first labour government embarked on a progressive programme of industrial development organised by the newly-formed Industrial Development Board (IDB). This organisation founded a number of factories with the goal of creating vertical linkages with the new agricultural sector. Thus, an edible oil factory produced cooking oil and animal feed from the cotton seeds; another factory produced the staple cornmeal from locally-grown corn; while another enterprise produced arrowroot; and a cotton ginnery served the Sea Island cotton industry of the Leeward Islands as the central location to gin the fine cotton and produce seeds for planting. Indeed, Antigua and Barbuda seemed to be firmly established on the road to progress with the formerly disenfranchised people at the helm of their own development.

The next stage of constitutional advancement was to come in 1967 with the status of Statehood in Association with Britain – a sort of halfway house to full independence – where the national

Prime Minister, Baldwin Spencer (left) and former Prime Minister, Lester Bird handing over a signed Code of Conduct governing the 2004 general elections to Chairman of the Antigua Christian Council, Bishop Donald J. Reece.
Photo: Maurice Merchant

Prime Minister, Baldwin Spencer speaking at a UPP rally to celebrate the first anniversary of his government in office.

Photo: Maurice Merchant

government was given responsibility for the state's internal affairs while Britain retained responsibility for defence and external affairs.

However, during the decade of the 1960s, a number of tensions developed in the AT&LU leading in 1968 to that organisation rupturing and a number of its influential leaders forming a new union – the Antigua Workers' Union (AWU). The leader of this new union, former General Secretary of the AT&LU, George Walter, would go on to help form a new political party – the Progressive Labour Movement (PLM) – that would challenge the Antigua Labour Party successfully in the general elections of 1971.

Thus, the decade of the 1970s opened with a new government in Antigua and Barbuda. While the early initiatives of the ALP had met with unqualified success, the new social forces unleashed by this very success proved problematic for the then ageing leadership of that party. Furthermore, the conflicts that developed as a result of the leadership of the union being, at the same time, the leadership of the national government proved difficult to resolve and contributed significantly to the loss of popularity and confidence that helped motivate the electorate to turn their allegiance to the new PLM party.

Notwithstanding their impressive victory at the polls, however, the new government was bedevilled by an international situation that undermined their efforts to grow the economy and empower the people. For it was at this time in the early 1970s that the global oil market was destabilised, with the advent of the OPEC oil cartel, the rapid increase in oil prices and the resultant shocks to the economies of small states in particular. Thus, the economic and social programmes of the PLM government were undermined by events over which they had no control.

The early 1970s also saw the emergence of a new political force called the Antigua Caribbean Liberation Movement (ACLM), led by prominent activist Leonard Tim Hector. Hector had emerged as a political strategist with the AWU during its struggle with the AT&LU and the ALP during the late 1960s. Later, however, as first Chairman of the PLM, he had clashed with George Walter, the AWU strongman who had decided to seize the opportunity to rise to national leadership as head of a PLM government.

Thus, outmanoeuvred by the erstwhile trade unionist, Hector, a respected intellectual and historian, organised his movement and dedicated his organisation to a certain brand of radical politics and to agitating against the PLM government. The mouthpiece of the ACLM, the weekly *Outlet* newspaper, proved an effective

propaganda tool and helped turn public opinion against the PLM regime.

The ALP, meanwhile, reorganised itself in opposition, attracting new blood and new competence into its leadership, in the shape of the leader's two sons, Vere Jr and Lester Bryant, both newly-qualified lawyers, and John St Luce, a graduate economist, along with Hugh Marshall. All four of these "Young Turks" had lived in England during the 1960s and had yearned to return home to participate in political activity. This reorganised and reenergized ALP became the people's choice at the 1976 elections, when it was returned to office with eleven of the seventeen seats in the Lower House of Parliament. One remarkable aspect of this result was the fact that three members of the Bird family – V.C. Bird Sr and his two sons, Vere Jr and Lester Bryant – were now all together members of parliament.

All the parties contesting the 1976 elections had stated their support for Antigua and Barbuda to become an independent nation during the ensuing parliamentary term. As it turned out, it was the ALP that won the opportunity to take the nation into independence in 1981. Independence Day on the 1 November 1981 marked the final break with the British colonial power, and the achievement of full independence for the nation that was officially named Antigua and Barbuda.

The new ALP regime was to govern the country for 28 years continuously until the elections of 2004, when a new political formation – the United Progressive Party (UPP) – would come to power in a landslide victory at the polls.

The first decade of independence was characterised by rapid economic growth that enhanced the popularity of the ALP regime. However, as the years went by, the new regime degenerated into a pattern of mismanagement of the economy that ultimately diminished its base of support and created the conditions that allowed for the emergence of a successful challenge to its leadership of the country.

The PLM that had lost the elections in 1976 continued to decline as a political force. A number of its leaders and supporters had come together in a new political grouping during the 1980s, called the United National Democratic Party (UNDP), led by prominent physician, Dr Ivor Heath. In the elections of 1989, the UNDP candidate for the St John's Rural West constituency, trade unionist Baldwin Spencer, was the only opposition candidate on Antigua to win a seat, with the ALP candidates being

Parliament in session.
Photo: Joseph Jones

victorious in all the other constituencies. Thus, with an impregnable majority in Parliament as the decade of the nineties opened, the ALP had returned to the kind of political hegemony it had enjoyed during the 1950s and early 1960s. Furthermore, the veteran ALP leader, Vere Bird Sr, was now of advanced age and was clearly no longer equal to the task of effectively steering the ship of state. Thus a leadership vacuum had opened at the highest level of state control. A struggle for power in the ALP was therefore imminent.

During 1990, a number of civil society organisations and the three opposition political parties (the PLM, UNDP, and the ACLM) began a series of consultations on the state of the political situation in the country. These consultations led to the formation of a coalition of organisations called the National Council of Organisations (NCO). During the year or so that the NCO lasted, its member organisations called for the unification of the opposition parties to confront the ALP hegemony. Out of this call resulted the formation of the United Progressive Party (UPP), a united front of the three opposition parties. Baldwin Spencer, the only member of any of these parties then in parliament was selected leader of the new united

party. At its first election challenge in 1994, the UPP gained five parliamentary seats, becoming the official opposition to the ALP, now led by V.C. Bird Sr's son, Lester Bryant.

The 1994 elections were a watershed that indicated clearly that the days of ALP leadership of the nation were numbered. A critical problem confronting the country, however, was the obsolete nature of the electoral system, with an electoral register that had not been revised in over two decades. The issue of electoral reform therefore became the rallying point of opposition forces. The ALP was not to yield on this issue until it had won yet another election in 1999, after which the calls for electoral reform became so strident that a new electoral system had to be implemented before the country would accept the legitimacy of any other elections.

Thus, the electoral system was reformed and a new electoral register was prepared by an Electoral Commission, a new institution in the management of national elections, during 2003. The stage was therefore set for the general elections of 2004 to be undoubtedly free and fair. These elections led to the first electoral defeat of the ALP in 28 years, and the accession to office of the United Progressive Party, with its leader Baldwin Spencer as Prime Minister.

Well-rounded and inclusive education system

ERMINA OSOBA

The education system in Antigua and Barbuda, a legacy of British colonialism, is basically structured along the lines of the British system. It is a three-tier system of primary, secondary and tertiary institutions. The first primary schools were established by various Christian denominations, particularly the Anglicans and the Moravians. Women have also played a critical role in the development of education in Antigua and Barbuda. Mention must be made of pioneers such as Nellie Robinson, Ernie Stevens and Hilda Davis who founded schools. The Thomas Oliver Robinson Memorial School started by Nellie Robinson, celebrated its 100th anniversary in 1998. The Foundation Mixed School, a primary school, founded by Hilda Davis in 1939, is still in existence.

Education is free and available to all children, and is compulsory up to the age of sixteen. The nation has a very young population with approximately 44 percent under the age of 25 years. The government, therefore, recognises that it has a mammoth task to educate its youth.

The current Minister of Education, the Honourable Bertrand Joseph has declared: "My Government is committed to expanding and enhancing our education system. With increasing globalisation and the CSME (Caribbean Single Market and Economy), the training and retraining of our human resources at all levels is critical. Of particular urgency is the expansion of secondary education. To this end, my Government has resolved to build two new secondary schools within its first five years in office."

Currently, the nation has 64 primary schools catering for children between the ages of five and twelve. Of this total, 34 are free; owned and operated by the government through its Ministry of Education. Some of the thirty private, fee-paying, primary schools follow international curricula. However, they must also incorporate basic elements of the national curriculum. There are six primary grades. On attaining Grade Six (at average age 11+) students sit a national Primary School Examination.

RIGHT
The graduating class of 2007 of the Bible Believers Foundation Pre-School.

Photo: Snapshots Imaging / M Henery

FACING PAGE
Foundation Mixed School is one of the country's 64 primary schools catering for children aged between five and twelve.

Photo: Joseph Jones

Successful candidates then progress to the next level of free, secondary education.

Of the sixteen secondary schools in the nation, nine are free, government-owned. Seven are fee-paying, private ones. Secondary school students range in age from eleven to eighteen years. They progress through five forms. In Form V, students sit for examinations of Caribbean Examinations Council (CXC) that cover a wide range of subjects. These examinations are roughly equivalent to the British GCE and A-level examinations, the European Baccalaureate, the American High School Diploma and the Canadian Grade 12.

The third tier in the system is the tertiary level. Today, there are four widely recognised institutions offering post-secondary, college and university level education as well as continuing education: The Antigua State College, the University of the West Indies School of Continuing Studies, the Antigua and Barbuda Hospitality Training Institute and the Antigua and Barbuda International Institute of Technology.

The oldest is the Government's Antigua State College that began as a teacher training college for the Leeward Islands. It now has several other departments including a post-secondary Advanced Level Department that prepares students for the Caribbean Examinations Council's CAPE examinations (equivalent to the Cambridge Advanced Level examinations). Its Undergraduate Department offers University of the West Indies accredited programmes in the Arts and Sciences. Departments of Engineering, Business and Commerce and Schools of Nursing and Pharmacy are also well established there.

TOP
Break time, and the chance to let off steam.
Photo: Joseph Jones

The University of the West Indies School of Continuing Studies, the outreach arm of UWI, caters to local needs for distance and continuing education. An important part of its stated mission is its commitment to the process of "continually enhancing the intellectual development of the Caribbean in all spheres".

The Antigua and Barbuda Hospitality Training Institute offers both academic and practical training for the Hospitality Industry. The Antigua and Barbuda International Institute of Technology is well on its way to becoming a regional institution of excellence in the field of information technology.

As a final note, it must be mentioned that pre-school education is fast becoming a critical sphere of the education system. Approximately 120 of such schools (including day-care centres) currently exist – all privately owned. However, several of the free, government primary schools have kindergarten sections attached to them. At this level, the teaching staff is 100 percent female. Indeed, the teaching profession in Antigua and Barbuda, as it is in many parts of the world today, is predominantly female.

TOP
Education is free to all children, and is compulsory up to the age of sixteen.
Photo: Joseph Martin

RIGHT
A school trip to ICT Fest in St John's provides access to new technology and the opportunity to show off gaming skills.
Photo: Joseph Jones

A flourishing media landscape

JOANNE C. HILLHOUSE

The big story in recent years, as far as media in Antigua is concerned, is greater access, specifically with respect to the radio airwaves. Still, a number of challenges – or shall we call them opportunities – remain. These include, but are not limited to, preserving press freedom and tempering that freedom with responsibility; creating greater diversity and balance; and producing more local content, more consistently.

The notion of media as the "voice" of the people is a fairly new chapter in a story that began in 1748, when the first publication reportedly came off the presses. Some would argue that it wasn't until 1943 with *The Workers Voice* that the notion of media for the masses began to take hold.

The next chapter would be characterised, in general, by media as a political tool – either via state control or protest. The Antigua Workers Union/Progressive Labour Movement answered the Antigua Trades & Labour Union/Antigua Labour Party's *Voice* with its *Antigua Star* in the late 1960s and 1970s; and the Antigua Caribbean Liberation Movement had its *Outlet*, with noted critic Leonard Tim Hector at its helm.

Others have come and gone over the years. Today, the front page belongs primarily to the *Daily Observer*, a publication that began as protest tool Observer by Fax in 1993 and blossomed into a widely read daily; and the *Antigua Sun*, yin to its yang, dating back to 1997. Both are privately owned, so too the small sample of special interest magazines.

Launched in 1943, *The Workers' Voice* took the first steps towards providing media for the masses

The most dramatic strides in the latter part of the 20th and early part of the 21st centuries, however, have surely been made by the electronic media; and, in particular, radio. Observer Radio, which began broadcasting literally at the dawn of the new millennium after a groundbreaking legal battle all the way to England's Privy Council, is credited with having played a critical role in the 2004 elections by

RIGHT
'Good Morning Antigua and Barbuda' is screened on ABS TV and features lifestyle issues as well as interviews with local artistes and entrepreneurs.

FACING PAGE
A news vendor plies his trade amid the busy traffic around the Antigua Recreation Ground.

Photos: Joseph Jones

dint of the unprecedented access it afforded other views.

State-owned ABS radio began broadcasting in the early 1960s, and, apart from the religious (Lighthouse) or relay stations (Caribbean Relay), radio remained, for a long time, the almost exclusive domain of the state. Though private, ZDK, licensed to operate in 1970, and its spin-off, SUN, were owned by and affiliated with the ruling government of the day.

Apart from breaking the state monopoly, Observer Radio altered the landscape in another significant way: In its wake, talk radio, largely non-existent before, quickly became the format of choice. Long silent, the public started talking and hasn't stopped, some moving around the dial on any given day from Observer to ZDK-cum-Liberty Radio (affiliated with the former Antigua Labour Party Government), to Crusader (owned by the now ruling United Progressive Party).

Given the various hues of ownership, it should be little surprise that politics tends to dominate.

But it hasn't all been chat. Music stations likes Family Radio and Red Hot, the latter owned by popular jam band Burning Flames, and GEM, which is regional but with a strong Antigua presence, have been joined by HITZ FM, Nice FM, and others.

Radio is almost certainly the medium of choice; no wonder then that even the local Catholic Church has hit the airwaves with its own station.

Television, meanwhile, is long overdue for a revolution. Broadcast from 1965 throughout the Leeward Islands and owned by Rediffusion International of London, Columbia Broadcasting, and Bermuda Radio and Television, ZAL was acquired by government in 1975 and renamed ABS-TV.

The Daily
"Let There Be Light"
OBSERVER

AntiguaSun
The Independent Newspaper of Antigua & Barbuda

Tim Hector was the editor of *The Outlet*, a publication which supported the Antigua Caribbean Liberation Movement. He died in 2002.

RIGHT
"Zugu" at the controls at Sun FM.
Photo: Joseph Jones

Cable Television Entertainment Systems hit the market in 1983, and enjoyed a monopoly for some time. Post-2004, the market was liberalised and Karib Cable, a regional company, entered the market. Both have local access stations, but the content, even on the

RIGHT
A sister publication to *The Daily Observer, Observer PM* is the latest newspaper to hit the stands.

state media is still largely foreign – and in particular, US-produced.

A number of independent producers – from Jah Tek to Cinque – have emerged in recent years, however, and though programme funding remains a challenge, continue to make their mark – from music video to commercial production. Notably, HAMA Productions, which has been producing TV programmes since the 1990s, recently upped the ante with the launch of its own station available to CTV subscribers.

It is noteworthy that more and more local producers and even established media are capitalising on the Internet. Sites like antiguanice.com have long been an online hub, primarily for potential visitors. Now, though, it is common for local stations (TV and radio) to stream online so that Antiguans and others abroad can keep up with happenings at home. Also, through the well-known video sharing and networking sites, not to mention individual web sites, music and video producers have found an even wider market for their product.

Added to the landscape in 2004, has been a fledgling media congress which, like the media itself, remains a work in progress.

Antigua-et-Barbuda : un petit bout de paradis

On disait autrefois de la petite société d'Antigua-et-Barbuda, dont les membres sont proches les uns des autres, que « Si l'on remonte assez loin dans le passé, tout le monde est parent avec tout le monde. » Aujourd'hui, ceux qui étaient partis sont revenus pour de grandes retrouvailles avec leur famille, et l'on voit ainsi certains habitants à la peau brune de la République dominicaine rejoindre la population traditionnelle noire, blanche ou arabe.

Il y a bien longtemps, nos grands-pères et leurs frères, en quête d'opportunités économiques, partirent à Saint-Domingue pour couper la canne à sucre. Dans la plupart des cas, on n'entendit plus jamais parler d'eux, jusqu'à ce que leurs descendants reviennent pour réclamer leur patrimoine. C'est pourquoi, dans les classes des écoles primaires, des Davis sont aujourd'hui assis à côté de Diaz, et des Pena sont amis avec des Peters.

Le samedi, les Antiguaises achètent au marché des légumes aux marchands dominicains, se rendent à pied dans les quartiers chics pour faire des courses dans des magasins libanais ou syriens, puis vont en grand nombre dans des salons de coiffure espagnols pour être bien coiffées le dimanche matin, avant d'aller chercher un plat chinois de chop suey au poulet ou de porc « jerk » à la jamaïcaine.

En avance de nombreuses années sur le mouvement d'intégration, cette nation formée de deux îles, d'une superficie de 440 km², est une société multiraciale et multi-ethnique issue de différentes nations.

Parmi les nouveaux immigrants (Espagnols, Chinois, Africains, Guyanais et Jamaïcains), on trouve des centaines d'Américains et d'Européens blancs, maintenant plus nombreux que les descendants, nés ici, de marchands portugais ou écossais. Certains, comme Christophe Colomb, sont venus en voyage de découverte, mais ont décidé de jeter l'ancre – souvent dans les petits ports pittoresques d'English Harbour, Falmouth ou Cobbs Cross dans le sud-est et, de plus en plus, de Jolly Harbour dans le sud-ouest.

La population, en pleine croissance, occupe maintenant toute l'île, et l'on trouve à présent des villages là où étaient jadis plantés des champs de canne à sucre et des pâturages pour les vaches. Les moulins abandonnés – seuls vestiges des anciennes plantations sucrières – témoignent du déclin de l'agriculture au profit d'autres industries nécessitant moins de main-d'œuvre comme la banque, l'assurance, les télécommunications et l'aéronautique, qui ont contribué à l'émergence d'une classe moyenne forte.

C'est toutefois le tourisme qui reste la principale industrie d'Antigua-et-Barbuda. Les nombreux hôtels – du prestigieux Curtain Bluff à l'hôtel Sandals de renommée mondiale, en passant par le Jolly Beach Resort (un établissement géré au niveau local qui est aussi la plus grande propriété du pays), ou encore les auberges VIP (very intimate places, ou lieux très intimes) – s'adressent à toutes les catégories de clientèle. Bénéficiant de la fraîcheur des alizés, ces îles inondées de soleil offrent certaines des plus belles plages du monde : 365 véritables joyaux au sable blanc à Antigua et des plages de rêve immaculées au sable rose à Barbuda. L'île sœur possède également un lagon très bien préservé qui abrite une réserve protégée où l'on trouve des frégates et une population de daims.

Grâce à l'aéroport international qui accueille de grandes compagnies aériennes comme American Airlines, Air Canada, British Airways et Virgin Atlantic, mais aussi des compagnies antillaises telles que LIAT et Caribbean Airlines, il est possible de se rendre facilement et directement à Antigua-et-Barbuda. Et pour le voyageur d'affaires, les équipements de télécommunications de pointe (tels que l'Internet haut débit et le téléphone international direct) et les installations pour conférences font quasiment des voyages d'affaires d'agréables vacances.

Quant aux passagers des paquebots de croisière, ils profitent de leur escale pour faire des achats dans les boutiques hors taxes du port de la capitale, pour dîner dans les nombreux et excellents restaurants, pour visiter des sites historiques comme les ruines du fort Shirley et Nelson's Dockyard (chantier naval de Nelson et son musée dans un bâtiment du XVIIIe siècle restauré) ; ils font aussi du cheval, nagent avec les raies pastenagues dans l'Atlantique ou longent la côte nord-est en kayak.

Le niveau de vie des habitants ayant augmenté, les activités de loisirs ont pris de l'ampleur et se sont diversifiées. Mais certaines distractions sont presque sacrées. Les Antiguais et les Barbudais de l'étranger viennent séjourner dans leur patrie en juillet et août, au moment du carnaval, que l'on qualifie de « plus grand festival d'été des Caraïbes ». Onze jours durant, Antigua s'amuse en célébrant cette fête avec des mascarades hautes en couleur, de la musique de steel band pleine d'énergie, des airs de calypso aux paroles douces et/ou satiriques et des danses de rue libératrices qui balaient d'un coup les différences de race, de religion ou de classe.

Pour le carnaval de Barbuda, appelé Caribana, qui a lieu plus tôt dans l'année et dont l'organisation est semblable à celui d'Antigua, les Antiguais vont à l'île sœur pour y passer un week-end agrémenté des saveurs du homard, du crabe, du lambi ou de la venaison.

Le moment où les arrivées par avion sont les plus nombreuses est sans doute le mois d'avril, époque où ont généralement lieu les matches internationaux de cricket et la Semaine de la voile. Le cricket, pratiqué sur un terrain qui a fait date dans l'histoire (l'Antigua Recreation Grounds), constitue un véritable festival en soi, où le fait de gagner ou de perdre n'est qu'un détail de ces journées de fête que l'on passe à boire, manger, rire et écouter de la musique. C'est ici que l'hospitalité et l'amabilité bien connues des Antiguais sont les plus visibles, comme vous le diront les passionnés qui reviennent chaque année.

Quant à la Semaine de la voile – où se dispute l'une des plus grandes régates du monde –, elle attire des amoureux de la voile des quatre coins de la planète, transformant ainsi English Harbour, Falmouth Harbour et Jolly Harbour en centres où règne une activité fébrile. Le Salon nautique de printemps, où sont présentés à Falmouth Harbour les bateaux les plus luxueux du monde, est un grand moment autant pour ceux qui achètent que pour ceux qui regardent émerveillés.

« Homecoming », le tout dernier festival, a été organisé pour la première fois en 2004 pour la fête de l'indépendance. Les festivités ont tourné autour de la fierté communautaire, des institutions et symboles nationaux, ainsi que d'événements historiques importants. Elles ont également été l'occasion de divertissements tels que des concours de beauté locaux, une fête du gospel et un banquet de gala où l'on pouvait danser. Vu le succès qu'a connu ce festival, il aura vraisemblablement lieu chaque année.

Les Antiguais et les Barbudais sont de tradition chrétienne, et quelle que soit l'heure à laquelle la fête du samedi soir s'est terminée, le nombre des fidèles présents à la messe du dimanche est en général élevé. Outre la cathédrale anglicane de Saint John's qui domine la ville, des églises de confession méthodiste, morave, catholique, adventiste, baptiste, wesleyenne, luthérienne et pentecôtiste coexistent pacifiquement avec des assemblées de fidèles moins nombreux comme les bahaïs, les musulmans et les hindous.

En plus d'être les gardiennes des âmes, les églises contribuent à préserver la culture. Les foires alimentaires anglicane et morave, par exemple, sont des manifestations nationales où la nourriture est tout autant exposée que consommée. C'est là que les communautés d'immigrants se réalisent pleinement, en offrant de délicieux plats aussi variés que les sushis japonais, le *mountain chicken* dominicain, le ragoût *kiddie* de Montserrat et la salsepareille (aphrodisiaque) de Saint-Kitts. Et des plats locaux très prisés comme le boudin au riz mariné, l'alose à la farine de maïs et le poisson salé au *doucana* (boulettes aux fruit secs) ne se conservent bien sûr que très peu de temps.

Ces manifestations ne permettent pas seulement aux églises de collecter de l'argent, elles nous donnent la possibilité de nous affirmer et nous rassurent sur le fait que, malgré la montée des valeurs nord-américaines, la télévision par câble et l'Internet, nous restons antillais là où cela compte, c'est-à-dire dans notre ventre, dans notre cœur et dans notre attitude.

Antigua-et-Barbuda - Faits et chiffres

Nom : Antigua-et-Barbuda

Capitale : Saint John's

Superficie et situation géographique : Antigua, la plus grande des îles Sous-le-Vent anglophones, mesure 23 km de long sur 18 km de large, pour une superficie d'environ 280 km². Le point le plus haut est Boggy Peak, qui s'élève à 402 m. Barbuda, située à quelque 48 km au nord d'Antigua, est une île corallienne plate d'une superficie d'à peu près 176 km².

Antigua-et-Barbuda se situe au milieu des îles Sous-le-Vent, dans l'est des Caraïbes, à 17 degrés environ au nord de l'équateur. Au sud, se trouvent les îles de Montserrat et de la Guadeloupe et, à l'ouest et au nord, Nevis, Saint-Kitts, Saint-Barthélemy et Saint-Martin.

Climat : les températures vont approximativement de 23° C en hiver à 29° C en été. Il pleut en moyenne 1 140 mm seulement par an, ce qui en fait les îles les plus ensoleillées des Caraïbes orientales, avec une faible humidité toute l'année.

Chef de l'Etat : la reine Elisabeth II, représentée par le gouverneur général Louise Lake-Tack

Premier ministre : Baldwin Spencer

Population : 69 481 habitants (2007)

Langue : anglais

Monnaie : dollar des Caraïbes de l'est (EC$) ; le dollar des Etats-Unis (US$) est également accepté

Indicatif international : +1 268

Domaine Internet : .ag

Electricité : dans une partie de l'île, le courant est de 110 volts et dans le reste, il est de 220 volts. La plupart des hôtels sont équipés pour les deux voltages.

Banques : Antigua and Barbuda Development Bank, Antigua and Barbuda Investment Bank, Antigua Commercial Bank, Bank of Antigua, Bank of Nova Scotia, First Caribbean International Bank, Global Bank of Commerce, RBTT Bank, Royal Bank of Canada.

Equipements médicaux : il y a un hôpital et une clinique privée, ainsi que de nombreux médecins généralistes et spécialistes. Des services de pharmacie sont disponibles partout sur les îles.

Passeport et immigration : les ressortissants des Etats-Unis, du Canada et de l'Union européenne doivent être en mesure de prouver leur nationalité (passeport en cours de validité ou extrait d'acte de naissance certifié conforme). Les résidents des autres pays doivent s'informer des formalités d'entrée auprès de l'office de tourisme le plus proche.

VOYAGES EN AVION

L'aéroport international V.C. Bird est le point d'entrée des voyageurs arrivant en avion à Antigua-et-Barbuda. Il existe des vols directs et des correspondances au départ de l'Amérique du Nord via San Juan et Saint-Martin, ainsi que plusieurs vols quotidiens depuis l'Europe. Des vols réguliers et charters desservent de nombreuses îles voisines.

Durée de vol : New York - 4 h ; Miami - 3 h ; Toronto - 4 h ; Puerto Rico - 1 h ; Londres - 8 h ; Francfort - 9 h ; Paris - 8 h.

Compagnies aériennes desservant l'Amérique du Nord : Air Canada, American Airlines, BWIA, Continental Airlines, US Air.

Compagnies aériennes desservant le Royaume-Uni : British Airways, Virgin Atlantic et Sunsail Airways, avec des correspondances vers l'Europe.

Compagnies assurant des vols inter-îles : LIAT, Air St Kitts/Nevis, Carib Aviation, Caribbean Airlines, Montserrat Airways.

VOYAGES EN BATEAU

Le port de Saint John's et Heritage Quay, au cœur de la capitale, peuvent accueillir les paquebots de croisière.

Offices DE TOURISME

Etats-Unis

Antigua and Barbuda Department of Tourism and Trade
25 S.E. 2nd Avenue, Suite 300, Miami, FL 33131

Tél. : 305-381-6762. Fax : 305-381-7908
Email : cganuear@bellsouth.net

Antigua and Barbuda Department of Tourism
610 Fifth Avenue, Suite 311, New York, NY 10020

Appel gratuit : 888-268-4227. Tél. : 212-541-4117
Fax : 212-541-4789. Email : info@antigua-barbuda.org

Embassy of Antigua and Barbuda
3216 New Mexico Avenue NW, Washington, DC 20016
Tél. : 202 362 5122. Fax : 202 362 5225
Email : embantbar@aol.com

Canada

Antigua and Barbuda Department of Tourism & Trade
60 St Claire Avenue East, Suite 304, Toronto, Ontario, M4T 1N5

Tél. : 416-961-3085. Fax : 416-961-7218
Email : info@antigua-barbuda-ca.com

Royaume-Uni

Antigua and Barbuda Department of Tourism
2nd Floor, 45 Crawford Place, London, W1H 4LP

Tél. : (44) 20 7258 0070. Fax : (44) 20 7258 7486
Site Internet : www.antigua-barbuda.com
Email : antbar@msn.com

Allemagne, Autriche, Suisse et Nord de l'Europe

Fremdenverkehrsamt Antigua und Barbuda
Thomasstr. 11, D-61348 Bad Homburg, Allemagne

Tél. : 49-6172-21504
Fax : 49-6172-21513

France

Office du Tourisme d'Antigua-et-Barbuda
43, avenue de Friedland, 75008 Paris

Tél. : 33 (0) 1 53 75 15 71
Fax : 33 (0) 1 53 75 15 69

Italie

Dipartimento del Turismo di Antigua e Barbuda
Via Santa Maria alla Porta, 9, 20123 Milan

Tél./fax : (039) 02 877 983
Tél. (pour les professionnels du voyage) : (039) 02 720 987 27

Antigua-et-Barbuda

Antigua and Barbuda Department of Tourism
Government Complex, Queen Elizabeth Highway, St John's

Tél. : 268-462-0480. Fax : 268-462-2483
Email : deptourism@antigua.gov.ag

Antigua Hotels & Tourists Association
Island House, New Gates Street, P.O. Box 454, St John's

Tél. : 268-462-0374. Fax : 268-462-3702
Email : ahta@candw.ag

Magasin rustique dans Redcliffe Quay / *Rustic shop in Redcliffe Quay*   Photo: Joseph Jones

Antigua und Barbuda: Ein Stückchen Paradies

Von der kleinen, eng verwobenen Gesellschaft Antiguas und Barbudas wurde früher gesagt: „Wenn man weit genug zurückgeht, sind *alle* miteinander verwandt". Inzwischen sind viele der ursprünglichen Verwandten aus anderen Gegenden zurückgekehrt, so dass sich braune Gesichter aus der Dominikanischen Republik unter die traditionell schwarze, weiße und arabische Bevölkerung mischen.

Auf der Suche nach Arbeit gingen vor langer, langer Zeit unsere Großväter und ihre Brüder nach Santo Domingo, um dort Zuckerrohr zu schneiden. Von vielen wurde nie wieder gehört, bis ihre Nachkommen heimkehrten, um ihr Geburtsrecht geltend zu machen. Die Namen verraten ihren Ursprung: In den Klassenzimmern der Grundschule sitzen heute Davis und Diaz nebeneinander und sind Pena und Peters beste Freunde.

Auf dem Samstagsmarkt feilschen Antiguanerinnen mit dominikanischen Verkäufern um Gemüse, gehen dann zum Einkaufen in libanesischen und syrischen Läden ins obere Stadtteil, lassen sich anschließend in spanischen Friseursalons ihre Sonntagsfrisur legen, bevor sie auf dem Heimweg ein Hähnchen Chop Suey oder ein jamaikanisches Jerk-Schweinefleisch-Gericht mitnehmen.

Allen Integrationsbewegungen um Lichtjahre voraus, ist dieser 440 Quadratkilometer große Doppelinselstaat, ohne viel Aufhebens darum zu machen, eine multinationale, multrassische Vielvölkergemeinschaft.

Unter den neueren Einwanderern – den Spaniern, Chinesen, Afrikanern, Guyanesen und Jamaikanern – befinden sich auch Hunderte von weißen Amerikanern und Europäern, die jetzt den hier gebürtigen Abkommen portugiesischer und schottischer Kaufleute zahlenmäßig überlegen sind. Manche kamen wie Kolumbus auf Entdeckungsreise, beschlossen aber auf Dauer vor Anker zu gehen – oft in den malerischen Fischerdörfern English Harbour/Falmouth/Cobbs Cross im Südosten und immer mehr auch in Jolly Harbour im Südwesten.

Die wachsende Bevölkerung hat sich über die Insel ausgebreitet und Gegenden besiedelt, die früher Zuckerrohrplantagen und Rinderweiden vorbehalten waren. Verlassene Windmühlen – die einzigen Überreste des ehemaligen Zuckeranbaus – sind Zeugen des Rückgangs der Landwirtschaft und des Aufkommens anderer, weniger arbeitsintensiver Industriezweige wie Bankwesen, Versicherungen, Telekommunikation und Luftfahrt, die dazu beigetragen haben, eine solide Mittelklasse entstehen zu lassen.

Der Tourismus ist und bleibt jedoch die Haupteinnahmequelle von Antigua und Barbuda, und es stehen zahlreiche Hotels für alle Besucherklassen zur Verfügung – vom exklusiven Curtain Bluff und dem weltberühmten Sandals über das lokal betriebene Jolly Beach Resort (der größten Hotelanlage des Landes) bis hin zu VIP-Gasthäusern (Very Intimate Places). Die von kühlenden tropischen Brisen umwehten, sonnengetränkten Inseln besitzen einige der spektakulärsten Strände der Welt: 365 weißsandige Kleinode auf Antigua und einsame Buchten mit rosarotem Sand auf Barbuda. Die Schwesterinsel kann sich auch einer unverdorbenen Lagune rühmen, die ein gut gehegtes Schutzgebiet für Fregattvögel und Damwild bildet.

Über seinen internationalen Flughafen, der von großen Fluggesellschaften wie American Airlines, Air Canada, British Airways und Virgin Atlantic sowie von karibischen Airlines wie LIAT und Caribbean Airlines angeflogen wird, ist Antigua und Barbuda einfach und direkt erreichbar. Und für Geschäftsreisende sorgen fortschrittliche Telekommunikationen (inkl. Broadband-Internet und internationale Telefon-Direktdurchwahl) und Konferenzeinrichtungen dafür, dass ihnen die Arbeit mehr wie Urlaub vorkommt.

Kreuzfahrtpassagiere nutzen unterdessen ihre Landausflüge zum Shopping in den Duty-Free-Läden der Hauptstadt, speisen in den vielen ausgezeichneten Restaurants, erkunden historische Stätten (z.B. die Ruinen von Fort Shirley, Nelson's Dockyard, ein restauriertes georgianisches Museum und einen Boatyard), gehen reiten, schwimmen mit Stachelrochen im Atlantik oder fahren an der Nordostküste Kajak.

Im Zuge des steigenden Wohlstands der Inselbewohner hat sich das Freizeitangebot vergrößert und diversifiziert. Gewisse Aktivitäten sind allerdings immer noch geradezu heilig. Im Ausland lebende Antiguaner und Barbudaner planen ihre Heimatbesuche vorwiegend für die Monate Juli und August, um beim Karneval – dem „großartigsten Sommerfest der Karibik" – mit dabei zu sein. Dann wird in Antigua elf Tage lang gefeiert – mit bunten Maskeraden, rhythmischen Steelbands, romantischen und/oder satirischen Calypsoliedern und kathartischen Straßentänzen, die alle Rassen-, Glaubens- und Klassenunterschiede beiseite fegen.

Für den ähnlich strukturierten Karneval von Barbudas, Caribana genannt, der früher im Jahr abgehalten wird, machen sich die Antiguaner zu ihrer Schwesterinsel auf, wo sie ein Wochenende köstlicher Schlemmerei mit Hummer, Krabben, Muscheln und Wildbret erwartet.

Die meisten Fluggäste kommen jedoch im April, der Zeit des Test Cricket und der Segelwoche. Cricket im historischen Antigua Recreation Grounds ist schon ein Festival für sich, bei dem die Entscheidung über Sieg oder Niederlage fast nebensächlich ist – angesichts der ganztägigen Partys, bei denen gegessen, getrunken, gelacht und viel Musik gemacht wird. Hier wird die berühmte antiguanische Gastfreundlichkeit besonders augenfällig, wie die Jahr um Jahr wiederkehrenden Fans bescheinigen werden.

Die Segelwoche ihrerseits – eine der führenden Regatten der Welt – lockt Yachties und Bootsliebhaber aus aller Welt an und macht English Harbour, Falmouth und Jolly Harbour zum Mittelpunkt fieberhafter Aktivitäten. Die Frühlings-Bootsschau, auf der in Falmouth Harbour die luxuriösesten Boote der Welt zu sehen sind, ist ein einzigartiges Erlebnis sowohl für Käufer als auch staunende Zuschauer.

Zum Unabhängigkeitstag wurde 2004 erstmalig ein neues Festival mit dem Namen „Homecoming" veranstaltet. Gefeiert wurden dabei der Stolz auf die eigene Gesellschaft, auf nationale Institutionen und Ikonen sowie wichtige historische Ereignisse. Zur Unterhaltung trugen Schönheitswettbewerbe, ein „Gospelfest" und ein Gala-Bankett mit Tanz bei. Aufgrund seines Erfolgs ist anzunehmen, dass das Festival zu einem jährlichen Event werden wird.

Die Antiguaner und Barbudaner sind traditionsgemäß Christen, und ganz egal bis wie spät in die Nacht hinein am Samstagabend gefeiert wurde, sind die Kirchen am Sonntagmorgen doch meist gut gefüllt. Zwar beherrscht die anglikanische Kathedrale von St. John's das Stadtbild, doch auch Methodisten, Moravianer, Katholiken, Adventisten, Baptisten, Wesleyaner, Lutheraner und Mitglieder der Pfingstgemeinden koexistieren friedlich miteinander und mit den kleineren Gemeinden der Baha'i, Moslemen und Hindus.

Die Kirche hütet jedoch nicht nur Seelen sondern trägt auch zur Bewahrung der Volkskultur bei. Die anglikanische und die moravische Lebensmittelmesse sind beispielsweise nationale Veranstaltungen, auf denen zu gleichen Teilen ausgestellt und verzehrt wird. Hier machen sich vor allem auch die Einwanderer nachdrücklich bemerkbar und bieten vielerlei Köstlichkeiten an – von japanischem Sushi über dominikanisches Berghuhn und montserratischen Ziegeneintopf bis hin zu Sarsaparilla, einem Aphrodisiakum der Kittitians. Natürlich wird auch bei lokalen Speisen wie Souse (gepökelte Schweinepfoten) mit Reis, Black Pudding (Blutwurst), Funghi (Maisbrei) und Shadfisch oder Doucana (Brei aus Kokosnüssen & Süßkartoffeln) mit Salzfisch kräftig zugelangt.

Diese Veranstaltungen dienen nicht lediglich der Spendenbeschaffung – sie sind vielmehr eine sehr reale Bestätigung für uns, dass wir trotz des Umsichgreifens nordamerikanischer Werte, trotz Kabelfernsehen und Internet immer noch da Westindier sind, wo es wirklich zählt – im Magen, Herzen und Geist.

Antigua & Barbuda - Fakten & Zahlen

Name: Antigua und Barbuda

Hauptstadt: St John's

Größe & Lage: Antigua, die größte der englischsprachigen Inseln über dem Wind, ist bei einer Fläche von zirka 280 km² etwa 23 km lang und 18 km breit. Der höchste Punkt der Insel ist Boggy Peak, der sich 402 m über dem Meeresspiegel erhebt. Barbuda, etwa 48 km nördlich von Antigua, ist eine flache Koralleninsel mit einer Fläche von zirka 176 km².

Antigua und Barbuda befinden sich in der Mitte der Inseln über dem Wind in der östlichen Karibik, etwa 17 Grad nördlich des Äquators. Südlich von ihnen liegen die Inseln Montserrat und Guadeloupe, nördlich und westlich liegen Nevis, St Kitts, St Barts und St Martin.

Klima: Die Temperaturen rangieren von zirka 23 Grad Celsius in den Wintermonaten bis zu zirka 30 Grad im Sommer. Der jährliche Niederschlag beträgt lediglich 114 cm, was die Inseln zu einer der sonnigsten Gegenden der östlichen Karibik mit ganzjährig niedriger Luftfeuchtigkeit macht.

Staatsoberhaupt: Königin Elizabeth II, vertreten durch den Generalgouverneur Louise Lake-Tack

Premierminister: Baldwin Spencer

Bevölkerung: 69.481 (2007)

Landessprache: Englisch

Währung: Ostkaribischer Dollar (EC$); US-Dollar (US$) werden ebenfalls akzeptiert.

Internationale Telefonvorwahl: +1268

Internet-Domäne: .ag

Netzspannung: 110 V in einigen Teilen der Inseln, ansonsten 220 V. Die meisten Hotels haben beide Netzspannungen.

Banken: Antigua and Barbuda Development Bank, Antigua and Barbuda Investment Bank, Antigua Commercial Bank, Bank of Antigua, Bank of Nova Scotia, First Caribbean International Bank, Global Bank of Commerce, RBTT Bank, Royal Bank of Canada.

Medizinische Versorgung: Es gibt ein Krankenhaus und eine Privatklinik sowie zahlreiche Allgemein- und Fachärzte. Apothekendienste stehen überall auf den Inseln zur Verfügung.

Reisepässe & Einreise: Staatsangehörige der USA, Kanadas und der EU benötigen einen Staatsbürgerschaftsnachweis (gültiger Reisepass oder Geburtsurkunde). Staatsangehörige anderer Länder sollten sich im Reisebüro nach den für sie geltenden Einreisebestimmungen erkundigen.

ANREISE AUF DEM LUFTWEG

Besucher, die mit dem Flugzeug in Antigua und Barbuda eintreffen, landen auf dem Flughafen V.C. Bird International. Er wird von Nordamerika aus sowohl direkt als auch über San Juan und St Martin angeflogen, und es gibt mehrere Flüge täglich aus/nach Europa. Zu vielen der Nachbarinseln bestehen Linien- und Charterflugverbindungen.

Flugzeiten: New York - 4 Stunden; Miami - 3 Stunden; Toronto - 4 Stunden; Puerto Rico - 1 Stunde; London - 8 Stunden; Frankfurt - 9 Stunden; Paris - 8 Stunden.

Airlines aus/nach Nordamerika: Air Canada, American Airlines, BWIA, Continental Airlines, US Air.

Airlines aus/nach GB: British Airways, Virgin Atlantic und Sunsail Airways mit Verbindungen in übrige Europa.

Airlines von/zu anderen Inseln: LIAT, Air St Kitts/Nevis, Carib Aviation, Caribbean Airlines, Montserrat Airways.

ANREISE AUF DEM SEEWEG

Anlegestellen für Kreuzfahrtschiffe befinden sich in St John's Harbour und Heritage Quay im Herzen der Hauptstadt.

FREMDENVERKEHRSBÜROS

Vereinigte Staaten

Antigua and Barbuda Department of Tourism and Trade
25 S.E. 2nd Avenue, Suite 300, Miami, FL 33131

Tel: 305-381-6762. Fax: 305-381-7908
E-Mail: cganuear@bellsouth.net

Antigua and Barbuda Department of Tourism
610 Fifth Avenue, Suite 311, New York, NY 10020

Gebührenfrei: 888-268-4227. Tel: 212-541-4117
Fax: 212-541-4789.   E-Mail: info@antigua-barbuda.org

Embassy of Antigua and Barbuda
3216 New Mexico Avenue NW, Washington, DC 20016

Tel: 202 362 5122. Fax: 202 362 5225
E-Mail: embantbar@aol.com

Kanada

Antigua and Barbuda Department of Tourism & Trade
60 St Claire Avenue East, Suite 304, Toronto, Ontario, M4T 1N5

Tel: 416-961-3085. Fax: 416-961-7218
E-Mail: info@antigua-barbuda-ca.com

Großbritannien

Antigua and Barbuda Department of Tourism
2nd Floor, 45 Crawford Place, London, W1H 4LP

Tél. : (44) 20 7258 0070. Fax : (44) 20 7258 7486
Website: www.antigua-barbuda.com
E-Mail: antbar@msn.com

Deutschland, Österreich, Schweiz & Nordeuropa

Fremdenverkehrsamt Antigua und Barbuda
Thomasstr. 11, D-61348 Bad Homburg

Tel: 49-6172-21504
Fax: 49-6172-21513

Frankreich

Office du Tourisme D'Antigua et Barbuda
43 Avenue de Friedland, Paris 75008

Tel: 33 (0) 1 53 75 15 71. Fax 33 (0) 1 53 75 15 69

Italien

Dipartimento del Turismo di Antigua e Barbuda
Via Santa Maria alla Porta, 9, 20123 Milan

Tel/Fax: (039) 02 877 983
Tel (für das Reisegewerbe): (039) 02 720 987 27

Antigua und Barbuda

Antigua and Barbuda Department of Tourism
Government Complex, Queen Elizabeth Highway, St John's

Tel: 268-462-0480
Fax: 268-462-2483
E-Mail: deptourism@antigua.gov.ag

Antigua Hotels & Tourists Association
Island House, New Gates Street, P.O. Box 454, St John's

Tel: 268-462-0374. Fax: 268-462-3702
E-Mail: ahta@candw.ag

Tranquil Wasser des fünf Insel-Hafens / *Tranquil waters of Five Islands Harbour*   Foto: T Sprague / Photogenesis

Antigua e Barbuda: un angolo di paradiso

Della piccola società interconnessa di Antigua e Barbuda si diceva una volta che «se si va sufficientemente indietro nel tempo, sono tutti parenti». Oggi questi parenti sono tornati per una grande rimpatriata. Ai volti tradizionalmente neri, bianchi e arabi della popolazione si mescolano oggi facce brune dalla Repubblica Dominicana.

Secoli fa i nostri nonni e i loro fratelli partirono per Santo Domingo in cerca di opportunità economiche, per tagliare la canna da zucchero. Di molti se ne persero le tracce finché non tornò a casa la loro prole per rivendicare la propria nazionalità. Oggi quindi nell'aula della scuola elementare troviamo Davis seduto davanti a Diaz, e Pena e Peters sono migliori amici.

Al mercato del sabato le donne antiguane comprano verdure dai rivenditori dominicani, fanno una passeggiata in centro per comprare dai negozi libanesi e siriani e poi si rivedono tutte dal parrucchiere spagnolo per farsi l'acconciatura della domenica, portandosi poi a casa un pasto di *chop suey* cinese o di carne di maiale alla giamaicana. Avendo anticipato di molti anni il movimento d'integrazione, questa nazione formata da due isole gemelle di 440 km^2 è, senza vantarsene, una comunità multinazionale, multietnica e multirazziale.

Tra i nuovi immigranti spagnoli, africani, guyanesi e giamaicani vi sono anche centinaia di americani e europei di carnagione bianca, che oggi superano in numero i discendenti nativi dei mercanti portoghesi e scozzesi, alcuni dei quali vennero, come Colombo, in viaggio di scoperta, e decisero di calare l'ancora qui, spesso nelle pittoresche comunità marinare di English Harbour/ Falmouth/Cobbs Cross a sud est, ma sempre di più anche a Jolly Harbour a sud ovest.

La popolazione crescente si è sparsa per tutta l'isola, creando comunità dove una volta esistevano solo campi di canna da zucchero e pascoli per le mucche. I mulini abbandonati – tutto quel che rimane oggi delle piantagioni di zucchero ormai liquidate – sono testimonianze del declino dell'agricoltura e della nascita di altri settori a uso di lavoro meno intensivo, come banche, assicurazioni, telecomunicazioni e aviazione, che hanno contribuito a creare una solida classe media.

Il settore economico principale di Antigua e Barduna rimane tuttavia il turismo. Il settore alberghiero, che comprende hotel esclusivi come Curtain Bluff e alberghi di fama mondiale come Sandals, ma anche centri di villeggiatura a gestione locale come il Jolly Beach Resort (la più grande proprietà del paese) e locande come VIP

(sigla inglese di «luoghi molti intimi») soddisfano qualsiasi categoria di visitatore. Rinfrescate dalle brezze marine dei Caraibi, queste isole inondate di sole sono la patria di spiagge tra le più spettacolari del mondo – 365 tesori di sabbia bianca sull'isola di Antigua e luoghi di evasione di sabbia rosa incontaminata a Barbuda. L'isola sorella vanta anche una laguna dall'ambiente incontaminato che ospita una riserva per fregate e una popolazione di daini.

Con un aeroporto internazionale utilizzato da grandi compagnie aeree come American Airlines, Air Canada, British Airways e Virgin Atlantic, oltre alle linee aeree dei Caraibi come LIAT e Caribbean Airlines, raggiungere e partire da Antigua e Barbuda è facile e diretto. Il viaggiatore di affari troverà un sistema di telecomunicazione avanzato - con accesso a Internet in banda larga e collegamenti telefonici internazionali in teleselezione – oltre a strutture per congressi che praticamente trasformano il lavoro in una vacanza.

I passeggeri delle navi crociera approfittano al massimo delle loro tappe per fare acquisti nel porto duty-free della capitale, pranzare negli ottimi ristoranti, visitare i luoghi storici come le rovine di Fort Shirley e Nelson's Dockyard, un museo georgiano restaurato con cantiere navale, fare passeggiate a cavallo, nuotare nelle acque dell'Atlantico con le pastinache o esplorare in kayak le coste del nord est.

Con la crescente ricchezza della popolazione locale si sono sviluppate e diversificate le attività del tempo libero ma alcuni passatempi rimangono pressoché sacri. Gli emigrati di Antigua e Barbuba che vivono all'estero si organizzano per visitare il loro paese di origine nei mesi di luglio e agosto, per coincidere con il Carnevale, che viene definito «il più grande festival estivo dei Caraibi». I festeggiamenti durano undici giorni e Antigua si trasforma in un grande ballo in maschera coloratissimo, animato dalla musica delle steel band, dai canti dolci e/o satirici del calypso e da danze in strada catartiche che spazzano via le differenze tra razze, religioni e ceti sociali.

Anche a Barbuda si svolge nei primi mesi dell'anno un carnevale con programma molto simile, denominato Caribana, e ogni anno per celebrarlo gli abitanti di Antigua si trasferiscono a Barbuda per un fine settimana al gusto di aragosta, granchio, strombo e carne di daino.

Aprile è probabilmente il miglior mese per arrivare in aereo, perché è l'epoca dell'anno in cui si svolge il torneo di cricket e una settimana di gare in barca a vela.

Le partite di cricket allo storico parco ricreativo di Antigua sono un autentico festival, dove le vittorie e le sconfitte sono aspetti secondari delle feste che durano tutto il giorno, accompagnate da fiumi di bibite, cibo, musica e risate. È proprio in questo ambiente che sono evidenti l'ospitalità e l'amichevolezza degli antiguani, come testimoniano i fans che ritornano anno dopo anno.

La Sailing Week – una delle regate più famose del mondo – attira gli appassionati della vela e della navigazione da diporto da tutto il mondo, trasformando i porti di English, Falmouth e Jolly in alveari di attività frenetica. Il salone navale primaverile, durante il quale vengono esposte nel porto di Falmouth le imbarcazioni più lussuose del mondo, è una favolosa esperienza, si per chi vuole acquistare che per chi può permettersi solo di ammirare.

"Homecoming," il più recente dei festival, si è svolto per la prima volta durante la giornata dell'indipendenza del 2004. Ha celebrato in particolare l'orgoglio delle comunità locali, le istituzioni e le icone nazionali e gli eventi storici più significativi. Il programma ha compreso anche concorsi di bellezza regionali, una festa di musica gospel e un banchetto di gala con danze. Sulla scia del successo riscontrato dalla manifestazione si prevede che questo festival diventerà un evento annuale.

Gli abitanti di Antigua e Barbuda sono tradizionalmente cristiani e non importa a che ora del mattino si sia conclusa la festa del sabato sera, l'affluenza alla messa di domenica è generalmente molto grande. Benché la città sia dominata dalla cattedrale anglicana di St. John, le chiese metodiste, moraviane, cattoliche, avventiste, battiste, wesleyane, luterane e pentecostali coesistono tranquillamente con altre denominazioni minori come baha'i, islamici e hindu.

Oltre al loro ruolo di protettrici delle anime, le chiese contribuiscono anche alla salvaguardia della cultura. Le fiere gastronomiche anglicane e moraviane, per esempio, sono manifestazioni nazionali nelle quali l'arte culinaria diventa per metà esposizione e per metà consumo. È in questo ambiente che le comunità di immigranti hanno davvero l'occasione di esibirsi, offrendo specialità come sushi giapponese, pollo di montagna dominicano, stufato di capretto di Montserrat, e salsapariglia, un afrodisiaco proveniente da St. Kitts. Naturalmente vi sono anche i piatti preferiti antiguani come il sanguinaccio di riso e maiale e l'alosa con fungie (farina di grano) e le doucana (gnocchetti di farina, patata dolce, cocco e uva passa) con il pesce salato che vanno sempre a ruba.

Queste manifestazioni non vengono organizzate solo per raccogliere fondi per beneficenza, sono anche delle occasioni di autoaffermazione, rassicurandoci che malgrado l'invasione dei valori nordamericani, della TV via cavo e di Internet, siamo ancora abitanti delle Indie Occidentali – nel cuore, nello spirito e nello stomaco.

Antigua e Barbuda – Informazioni generali

Nome: Antigua e Barbuda

Capitale: St John's

Superficie e Posizione: La più grande delle Isole di Sottovento di lingua inglese, Antigua è lunga circa 23 km e larga 18 km, con una superficie di circa 280 km². Il punto più alto è Boggy Peak, che si eleva fino a 402 metri. Barbuda si trova a circa 48 km a nord di Antigua ed è un'isola piatta e corallina con una superficie di circa 176 km².

Antigua e Barbuda si trovano al centro delle Isole di Sottovento, nel Mar dei Caraibi orientale, a circa 17 gradi a nord dell'Equatore. A sud vi sono le isole di Montserrat e Guadeloupe, mentre a nord e a ovest vi sono Nevis, St Kitts, St Barts e St Martin.

Clima: la temperatura oscilla tra 23°C circa in inverno e 30°C circa in estate. La precipitazione annuale è in media di soli 114 cm, il che la rende la più soleggiata delle isole dei Caraibi orientali, con umidità bassa in tutto l'arco dell'anno.

Capo di stato: La regina Elisabetta II, rappresentata dal Governatore Generale Louise Lake-Tack

Primo ministro: Baldwin Spencer

Popolazione: 69.481 (2007)

Lingua: inglese

Valuta: dollaro dei Caraibi orientali (EC$), ma si possono utilizzare anche dollari statunitensi (US$)

Prefisso telefonico internazionale: +1268

Dominio Internet: .ag

Elettricità: in parte dell'isola è di 110 volt, nel resto dell'isola è di 220 volt. La maggior parte degli alberghi offre entrambi i voltaggi.

Banche: Antigua and Barbuda Development Bank, Antigua and Barbuda Investment Bank, Antigua Commercial Bank, Bank of Antigua, Bank of Nova Scotia, First Caribbean International Bank, Global Bank of Commerce, RBTT Bank, Royal Bank of Canada.

Strutture mediche: vi sono un ospedale e una clinica privata, oltre a numerosi medici di famiglia e specialisti. Sono disponibili servizi farmaceutici in tutte le isole.

Passaporti e immigrazion: I cittadini statunitensi, canadesi e dell'UE hanno bisogno di una prova di cittadinanza (passaporto valido o certificato di nascita autenticato). Ai cittadini di altre paesi si consiglia di contattare il più vicino ufficio turistico per informazioni sull'ammissione al paese.

ARRIVO IN AEREO

L'aeroporto internazionale V.C. Bird è il punto di entrata per i visitatori che arrivano in volo a Antigua e Barbuda. Vi sono sia voli diretti che coincidenze per l'America del Nord tramite San Juan e St Martin, oltre a vari voli giornalieri per l'Europa. Sono disponibili collegamenti charter e di linea per raggiungere molte delle isole vicine.

Tempi di volo: New York - 4 ore; Miami - 3 ore; Toronto - 4 ore; Puerto Rico - 1 ora; Londra - 8 ore; Francoforte - 9 ore; Parigi - 8 ore.

Linee aeree di collegamento con l'America del Nord: Air Canada, American Airlines, BWIA, Continental Airlines, US Air.

Linee aeree di collegamento con il Regno Unito: British Airways, Virgin Atlantic, e Sunsail Airways con coincidenze per l'Europa.

Linee aeree di collegamento tra le isole: LIAT, Air St Kitts/Nevis, Carib Aviation, Caribbean Airlines, Montserrat Airways.

ARRIVO VIA MARE

I porti per le navi da crociera sono a St John's Harbour e Heritage Quay, nel cuore della capitale.

UFFICI TURISTICI

Stati Uniti

Antigua and Barbuda Department of Tourism and Trade
25 S.E. 2nd Avenue, Suite 300, Miami, FL 33131

Tel: 305-381-6762. Fax: 305-381-7908
Email: cganuear@bellsouth.net

Antigua and Barbuda Department of Tourism
610 Fifth Avenue, Suite 311, New York, NY 10020

Chiamata gratuita: 888-268-4227
Tel: 212-541-4117. Fax: 212-541-4789
Email: info@antigua-barbuda.org

Ambasciata di Antigua e Barbuda
3216 New Mexico Avenue NW, Washington, DC 20016

Tel: 202 362 5122. Fax: 202 362 5225
Email: embantbar@aol.com

Canada

Antigua and Barbuda Department of Tourism & Trade
60 St Claire Avenue East, Suite 304, Toronto, Ontario, M4T 1N5

Tel: 416-961-3085. Fax: 416-961-7218
Email: info@antigua-barbuda-ca.com

Regno Unito

Antigua and Barbuda Department of Tourism
2nd Floor, 45 Crawford Place, London, W1H 4LP

Tél. : (44) 20 7258 0070. Fax : (44) 20 7258 7486
Sito web: www.antigua-barbuda.com
Email: antbar@msn.com

Germania, Austria, Svizzera e Europa del nord

Fremdenverkehrsamt Antigua und Barbuda
Thomasstr. 11, D-61348 Bad Homburg, Germania

Tel: 49-6172-21504
Fax: 49-6172-21513

Francia

Office du Tourisme D'Antigua et Barbuda
43 Avenue de Friedland, Parigi 75008

Tel: 33 (0) 1 53 75 15 71. Fax 33 (0) 1 53 75 15 69

Italia

Dipartimento del Turismo di Antigua e Barbuda
Via Santa Maria alla Porta, 9, 20123 Milano

Tel/Fax: (039) 02 877 983
Tel (per operatori turistici): (039) 02 720 987 27

Antigua e Barbuda

Antigua and Barbuda Department of Tourism
Government Complex, Queen Elizabeth Highway, St John's

Tel: 268-462-0480. Fax: 268-462-2483
Email: deptourism@antigua.gov.ag

Antigua Hotels & Tourists Association
Island House, New Gates Street, P.O. Box 454, St John's

Tel: 268-462-0374. Fax: 268-462-3702
Email: ahta@candw.ag

Tramonto dopo un altro giorno perfetto in Antigua / *Sunset after another perfect day in Antigua*   Foto: Antigua and Barbuda Tourism Department

Antigua y Barbuda: un trocito de paraíso

De la sociedad de Antigua y Barbuda, tan reducida y estrechamente ligada, se solía decir: "Si te remontas lo suficiente en el tiempo, *todo el mundo* está emparentado". Hoy en día, los familiares han vuelto para un gran reencuentro, y las morenas caras de la República Dominicana se mezclan con las de la población tradicional negra, blanca y árabe.

Volvamos a los tiempos en que nuestros abuelos y sus hermanos viajaron a Santo Domingo, buscando mejorar sus economías, para cortar la caña de azúcar. De muchos no se volvió a saber, hasta que sus hijos regresaron a casa para reclamar sus derechos de nacimiento. Y así, en las aulas de las escuelas primarias, Davis se sienta delante de Díaz, y Pena y Peters son amigos inseparables.

En el mercado de los sábados, las mujeres antiguanas compran verduras en los puestos de dominicanos, o caminan hasta las tiendas libanesas y sirias de la ciudad. Más tarde acuden en tropel a las peluquerías hispanas a arreglarse el pelo para el domingo por la mañana, no sin antes recoger una cena preparada de *chop suey* de pollo chino o de cerdo jamaicano al estilo *jerk*.

A años luz del movimiento integrador, esta nación de 274 kilómetros cuadrados y compuesta de dos islas es, sin bombo ni platillo, una comunidad multinacional, multiétnica y multirracial.

Entre los nuevos inmigrantes –hispanos, chinos, africanos, guyaneses y jamaicanos– se cuentan cientos de americanos y europeos blancos, que ya sobrepasan en número a los descendientes nacidos en la isla de mercaderes portugueses y escoceses. Algunos que, como Colón, llegaron en viajes de descubrimiento, optaron por echar el ancla, con frecuencia en las pintorescas comunidades marineras de English Harbour/Falmouth/Cobbs Cross en el sureste y, cada vez más, en Jolly Harbour en el sudoeste.

Esta pujante población se ha expandido por toda la isla, creando comunidades donde antes había cañaverales y pastos para el ganado. Los molinos abandonados –lo único que queda de las desaparecidas fincas de la caña de azúcar– son testimonio del decline de la agricultura y el auge de otras industrias menos laboriosas, como la banca, los seguros, las telecomunicaciones y la aviación, las cuales han contribuido a la consolidación de la clase media.

Sin embargo, el turismo sigue siendo la principal industria de Antigua y Barbuda, y sus numerosos hoteles satisfacen a todos los tipos de visitantes –desde el exclusivo *Curtain Bluff* y el mundialmente famoso *Sandals*, hasta el *Jolly Beach Resort* (gestionado localmente y el mayor bien inmueble del país) y los hospedajes *VIP* (*Very Intimate Places*). Las islas, refrescadas por brisas tropicales y bañadas por el sol, albergan algunas de las playas más espectaculares del mundo –365 gemas de blancas arenas en Antigua e inmaculados retiros de arenas rosas en Barbuda. La isla hermana también alardea de una laguna ecológica que acoge un santuario bien conservado de pájaros fragata y una población de gamos.

Llegar y salir de Antigua y Barbuda es fácil y directo. Su aeropuerto internacional es utilizado por algunas de las principales líneas aéreas como *American Airlines*, *Air Canada*, *British Airways* y *Virgin Atlantic*, además de por otras aerolíneas caribeñas como *LIAT* y *Caribbean Airlines*. Y para el viajero de negocios, las telecomunicaciones avanzadas –incluido Internet de banda ancha y telefonía internacional de marcado directo– y las instalaciones para conferencias, contribuyen a que hacer negocios sea casi una vacación.

Los pasajeros de los cruceros, por otro lado, sacan buen provecho de sus paradas comprando en el puerto libre de impuestos de la capital; comiendo en alguno de sus muchos excelentes restaurantes; explorando lugares históricos como las ruinas de Fort Shirley y Nelson´s Dockyard, un museo y astillero georgiano restaurado; montando a caballo; nadando entre rayas venenosas en el Atlántico; o bordeando la costa nordeste en kayak.

A medida que el nivel de vida de los lugareños ha ido subiendo, las actividades de ocio han aumentado y se han diversificado. Pero algunas fiestas siguen siendo casi sagradas. Los antiguanos y barbudenses que viven en el extranjero planean sus viajes a casa durante julio y agosto para coincidir con el Carnaval, calificado como "el mayor festival veraniego del Caribe". Durante más de once días, Antigua se deleita en una celebración de coloridas máscaras, vigorizante música de bandas de percusión típicas del Caribe, himnos de calipso melodiosos y/o satíricos, y catárticas danzas callejeras que borran de un plumazo las diferencias de raza, fe y clase.

Caribana, el carnaval de Barbuda, tiene una estructura similar y se celebra más temprano. Los antiguanos se trasladan a la isla hermana para celebrarlo y pasar un fin de semana aderezado con una variedad de langosta, cangrejo, concha y venado.

Quizá abril sea el mes con más visitantes, pues se suele celebrar entonces el *Test Cricket* y la Semana de la

Vela. El críquet en los históricos *Recreation Grounds* de Antigua es de por sí un festival, y ganar o perder es sólo un acompañamiento de las largas fiestas donde fluyen las libaciones, la comida, la risa y la música. Es aquí donde la famosa hospitalidad y simpatía antiguanas se ponen de mayor manifiesto, como atestiguan los aficionados que vuelven un año detrás de otro.

Por otro lado, la Semana de la Vela –una de las principales regatas del mundo– atrae regatistas y entusiastas de las embarcaciones de todos los lugares del mundo, transformando los puertos de English, Falmouth y Jolly en verdaderos hervideros de actividad. El *Boat Show* de primavera, cuando los barcos más lujosos del mundo se exhiben en Falmouth Harbour, es toda una experiencia para los compradores y los maravillados espectadores.

Homecoming, el más reciente de los festivales, se introdujo en el Día de la Independencia de 2004. La celebración se centró en el orgullo de la comunidad, las instituciones e iconos nacionales y en importantes eventos históricos. También tuvo actividades como concursos de belleza por zonas, un festival de *gospel*, y un banquete y baile de gala. Debido a su éxito, se espera que se convierta en un evento anual.

Los antiguanos y barbudenses son de tradición cristiana, e independientemente de hasta qué horas de la mañana dure la fiesta nocturna del sábado, la asistencia a la iglesia el domingo suele ser masiva. Si bien la catedral anglicana de St John´s domina la ciudad, las iglesias metodista, morava, católica, adventista, baptista, de Wesley, luterana y de Pentecostés conviven pacíficamente con congregaciones más pequeñas como las bahai, musulmana e hindú.

Además de ser las guardianas de las almas, las iglesias juegan su papel a la hora de conservar la cultura. Las ferias de comida anglicana y morava, por ejemplo, son acontecimientos nacionales en los que el arte culinario participa tanto de la exhibición como de la consumición. Es entonces que las comunidades de inmigrantes muestran lo mejor de sí mismas, ofreciendo delicias tan variadas como el *sushi* japonés, el pollo montañero dominicano, el estofado *kiddie* de Montserrat y la zarzaparrilla, un afrodisíaco de los habitantes de St Kitts. Por supuesto, no faltan los preferidos del lugar que, como la morcilla de arroz marinada; el fungie (una mezcla de harina de maíz y kimbombó) con el sábalo, y la doucana (bolas de harina y fruta seca) con salazones de pescado, duran nada y menos.

Estos acontecimientos no sirven sólo para recaudar fondos para las iglesias, sino que son indiscutibles autoafirmaciones, confirmaciones de que, a pesar de la invasión de los valores norteamericanos, la televisión por cable e Internet, aún somos antillanos ahí donde realmente cuenta: en el estómago, el corazón y el espíritu.

Antigua y Barbuda – Datos generales

Nombre: Antigua y Barbuda

Capital: St John's

Tamaño y ubicación: Antigua es la mayor de las Islas Leeward de habla inglesa. Tiene 23 km de largo, 18 km de ancho y un área aproximada de 174 km². Su punto más alto, Boggy Peak, se eleva 402 m. Barbuda está situada a unos 48 km al norte de Antigua y es una isla de coral llana con un área aproximada de 109 km².

Antigua y Barbuda está situada en el centro de las Islas Leeward en el Caribe Oriental, aproximadamente a 17 grados al norte del ecuador. Al sur están las islas de Montserrat y Guadalupe, y al norte y al oeste están Nevis, St Kitts, St Barts y St Martin.

Clima: Las temperaturas varían de alrededor de los 21 grados centígrados en los meses de invierno, a los algo menos de 30 en verano. Las precipitaciones anuales son de un promedio de 114 cm, lo cual la convierte en la más soleada de las islas del Caribe Oriental, con escasa humedad en cualquier época el año.

Jefe de Estado: La reina Isabel II, representada por el gobernador general Louise Lake-Tack

Primer Ministro: Baldwin Spencer

Población: 69.481 (2007)

Idioma: Inglés

Moneda: Dólar del Caribe Oriental (EC$); también se aceptan dólares estadounidenses (US$)

Código telefónico internacional: +1268

Dominio de internet: .ag

Electricidad: En parte de la isla hay 110 voltios, y en el resto 220. La mayoría de los hoteles tienen los dos voltajes.

Bancos: *Antigua and Barbuda Development Bank*, *Antigua and Barbuda Investment Bank*, *Antigua Commercial Bank*, *Bank of Antigua*, *Bank of Nova Scotia*, *First Caribbean International Bank*, *Global Bank of Commerce*, *RBTT Bank*, *Royal Bank of Canada*.

Servicios médicos: Existe un hospital y una clínica privada, así como numerosos médicos de cabecera y especialistas. Hay farmacias por toda la isla.

Pasaportes e inmigración: Los ciudadanos de los EE UU, Canadá y la Unión Europea necesitan prueba de ciudadanía

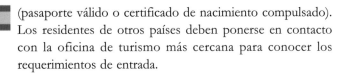

(pasaporte válido o certificado de nacimiento compulsado). Los residentes de otros países deben ponerse en contacto con la oficina de turismo más cercana para conocer los requerimientos de entrada.

VUELOS

El aeropuerto internacional *V.C. Bird* es el punto de entrada para los visitantes que llegan en avión a Antigua y Barbuda. Hay tanto vuelos directos como conexiones con Norteamérica vía San Juan y St Martin, y varios vuelos diarios desde Europa. También hay vuelos regulares y chárter a muchas de las islas vecinas.

Tiempos de vuelo: Nueva York - 4 h; Miami - 3 h; Toronto - 4 h; Puerto Rico - 1 h; Londres - 8 h; Francfort - 9 h; París - 8 h.

Aerolíneas desde Norteamérica: *Air Canada, American Airlines, BWIA, Continental Airlines, US Air.*

Aerolíneas desde el Reino Unido: *British Airways, Virgin Atlantic,* y *Sunsail Airways* con conexiones a Europa.

Aerolíneas entre las islas: *LIAT, Air St Kitts/Nevis, Carib Aviation, Caribbean Airlines, Montserrat Airways.*

NAVEGACIÓN

Los puertos para los cruceros están situados en St John's Harbour y Heritage Quay, en el corazón de la capital.

OFICINAS DE TURISMO

Estados Unidos

Departamento de Turismo y Comercio de Antigua y Barbuda
25 S.E. 2nd Avenue, Suite 300, Miami, FL 33131

Tfno: 305-381-6762
Fax: 305-381-7908
Email: cganuear@bellsouth.net

Departamento de Turismo de Antigua y Barbuda
610 Fifth Avenue, Suite 311, Nueva York, NY 10020

Número gratuito: 888-268-4227
Tfno: 212-541-4117
Fax: 212-541-4789
Email: info@antigua-barbuda.org

Embajada de Antigua y Barbuda
3216 New Mexico Avenue NW, Washington, DC 20016

Tfno: 202 362 5122. Fax: 202 362 5225
Email: embantbar@aol.com

Canadá

Departamento de Turismo y Comercio de Antigua y Barbuda
60 St Claire Avenue East, Suite 304, Toronto, Ontario, M4T 1N5

Tfno: 416-961-3085. Fax: 416-961-7218
Email: info@antigua-barbuda-ca.com

Reino Unido

Antigua and Barbuda Department of Tourism
2nd Floor, 45 Crawford Place, London, W1H 4LP

Tél. : (44) 20 7258 0070. Fax : (44) 20 7258 7486
Website: www.antigua-barbuda.com
Email: antbar@msn.com

Alemania, Austria, Suiza y Norte de Europa

Fremdenverkehrsamt Antigua und Barbuda
Thomasstr. 11, D-61348 Bad Homburg, Alemania

Tfno: 49-6172-21504. Fax: 49-6172-21513

Francia

Office du Tourisme D'Antigua et Barbuda
43 Avenue de Friedland, París 75008,

Tfno: 33 (0) 1 53 75 15 71. Fax 33 (0) 1 53 75 15 69

Italia

Dipartimento del Turismo di Antigua e Barbuda
Via Santa Maria alla Porta, 9, 20123 Milán,

Tfno/Fax: (039) 02 877 983
Tfno (para viajes de negocios): (039) 02 720 987 27

Antigua y Barbuda

Departamento de Turismo de Antigua y Barbuda
Government Complex, Queen Elizabeth Highway, St John's

Tfno: 268-462-0480. Fax: 268-462-2483
Email: deptourism@antigua.gov.ag

Asociación de Turistas y Hoteles de Antigua
Island House, New Gates Street, P.O. Box 454, St John's

Tfno: 268-462-0374. Fax: 268-462-3702
Email: ahta@candw.ag

Árboles magníficos del coco en la bahía de Morris / *Magnificent coconut palms at Morris Bay*   Foto: Joseph Jones

1797 年修造，这些石柱子是非常保留小船房子和风帆顶楼在纳尔逊的造船厂 Built in 1797, these stone pillars are all that remains of the boat house and sail loft at Nelson's Dockyard   Photo: Joseph Jones

安提瓜和巴布达：天堂一隅

安提瓜和巴布达，人口不多，彼此关系友好亲切，大家总爱说：'若要寻根问祖，个个都是自家人呢。'时至今日，亲朋好友每有团圆喜庆欢聚一堂时，但见融合着多个族裔，有多米尼加共和国棕色面孔，亦有传统黑人、白人以及阿拉伯族裔等，仿如小联合国。

回说当年，我们的一些祖父先辈为了寻找经济发展机会，远赴圣多明哥开采蔗园，很多人从此音讯杳然，直至一些后人重返故土，并带来众多源自西班牙语的名字，于是学校内英语名字的学生与西班牙语名字的学生成为好朋友的现象比比皆是，大家融洽地生活。

在周末市场，安提瓜妇女们要么光顾多米尼加人开设的小摊档，要么逛过黎巴嫩人或叙利亚人的店铺，然后光顾西班牙人的发廊为参与星期日早上的教堂聚会而美容一番，再到华人开设的鸡肉杂碎外卖店或牙买加人的烤肉食肆购买饭菜。

很久以前，这个占地 170 平方英哩（440 平方公里）的双岛之国，已经沉沉实实地建立了一个多国多种族人士聚居的融洽社会，而且彼此水乳交融。

新近移居此地的人士，除西班牙人、华人、非洲人、圭亚那人、牙买加人外，也有为数不多几百

无论如何，旅游业仍是安提瓜和巴布达最大的行业，各地酒店林立，接待各个阶层的游客。由顶级酒店 Curtain Bluff，享誉全球的 Sandals，以至本地经营的 Jolly Beach Resort（本地最大型物业），还有以亲切待客著称的名为 VIP 的小酒店，正是样样俱全。这里阳光灿烂、充满热带风情的小岛，拥有着闻名世界的美丽海滩 -- 安提瓜的洁白沙滩胜地和巴布达纯净、淡红的沙滩美景，一共不下 365 处。而后者亦以富有环保特色的礁湖驰名，无数军舰鸟候鸟群在那里栖息，而大量黄占鹿也都遍野皆是。

到安提瓜和巴布达旅游，直航交通非常方便，进出此间国际机场的各大航空公司不胜枚举，有美航、加航、英航及维珍航机，而加勒比海各航班如 BWIA、LIAT 及 Caribbean Star 亦定期来往各地。对于商务旅客来说，先进的通信设备，包括宽带网络及直拨国际长途电话等，以及会议设

名美国白人和欧洲白人，而他们说起来在人数比在这里土生土长的葡萄牙及苏格兰商人的后代还多。正如当年哥伦布发现新大陆之旅一样，有些人士路过此地就毅然留下来，在东南面 English Harbour/Falmouth/Cobbs Cross 一带，以及愈来愈多地在西南部 Jolly Harbour 等地风光美丽如画的渔业社会过着新生活。

人口正在不断蓬勃发展，逐渐散居全岛各地，昔日的甘蔗园及牧牛场已告湮没。竖立在荒废蔗园硕果仅存的一些古老风车，正见证着农业衰落，代之而起的是各式各类不那么劳动密集型的行业，诸如银行、保险、通信及航空业，随而也出现了一个稳固的中产阶级。

在东加勒比群岛各国中，安提瓜和巴布达于 1983 年率先与中华人民共和国建立外交关系。自从那时起两国关系良好，在国际舞台上相互支持。多年来，中国总共提供了 3.3 亿元人民币的援助，资助了许多建设项目如多功能文化与展览中心、YASCO 运动中心、Greekside 大桥，以及在 Darkwood 的高速公路改进工程。在新的相互合作协议中，中国将资助安提瓜和巴布达，建造一个新的板球运动场，该运动场工程将在 2007 年板球世界杯举行前竣工。预期两国关系将在平等互利的基础上得到继续发展，并为两国人民带来更多的福祉。

施，都能使阁下寓旅游于工作中，真是一举两得。

邮轮游客更大可趁途经此地在首都的免税码头轻松购物，既可在那里众多一流餐馆享受美食佳肴，亦可遨游 Fort Shirley 的历史古堡遗迹以及精心保存的乔治亚时代博物馆船厂 Nelson's Dockyard；又可骑马驰骋，在大西洋跟黄绍鱼一起戏水游泳，或在东北海岸划独木舟，各得其所。

随着本地居民生活日渐富裕，休闲活动也愈来愈见多采多姿。然而，人们对某些娱乐消遣始终一直乐此不疲，而且历久不衰。旅居国外的安提瓜人和巴布达人士喜爱于每年七八月间回国，藉以欢度嘉年华节。这被称为"加勒比海最大的夏季节期"，前后十一天，安提瓜到处一片欢腾，众人都别出心裁精心粉墨装扮，活力充沛的钢鼓乐随处可闻，而加力骚韵律的音乐则时而悠扬悦耳，时而讥刺热烈，往往令人捧腹大笑；街头巷

2004 年 11 月安提瓜和巴布达总理 W. Baldwin Spencer 对中国进行官方访问时与中国驻安巴大使任小平在长城合影。

由中国援助修建的中国-安提瓜和巴布达友谊大桥

由中国援助修建的中国-安提瓜和巴布达友谊大桥

中国驻安巴大使任小平会晤安巴驻中国大使 David Shoul。

尾都见大跳宣泄狂热的舞蹈，不分种族信仰和阶级，人人都玩过痛快。

而巴布达亦有同类性质的在年初举行的嘉年华节，称为'加勒比嘉年华'(Caribana)。安提瓜人纷纷奔往这姊妹岛欢度周末，饱餐一顿精选大螯虾、鲜蟹、海螺或鹿肉美食。

在四月间，此间的航班大概最为繁忙的了。木球大赛和帆船比赛周往往都在这时举行。在屡创佳绩的安提瓜康乐场 (Antigua Recreation Grounds)，不但木球赛事本身大受捧场，而且不论赢输，整日的杯觥交错，美食佳肴和悠扬乐韵等各类聚会活动，已足以令人乐而忘返。安提瓜人素有热情好客的美誉，在此更加表露无遗，难怪球迷们年年都乐于旧地重游。

帆船比赛周 -- 世界主要帆船大赛之一 -- 吸引全球各地赛帆运动好手及赛迷纷纷前来，English Harbour、Falmouth Harbour 和 Jolly Harbour 各个港口地区到处洋溢着一片欢乐气氛。同时，在 Falmouth Harbour 亦举行展出全球最豪华游艇的春季船展，对于富豪买家以至看得着迷的参观人士说来，都会是一次难得的体验。

最新的节庆"回家节"是在 2004 年独立日首次举行的。庆祝活动主题环绕社群尊严、国家传统和标志、以及各个深具意义的历史事件。此外，回家节亦举办各项娱乐活动，包括分区选美、福音演唱会及大型餐舞会。鉴于节庆活动圆满成功，预料今后将会年年都举行。

安提瓜人和巴布达人传统上信奉基督教，所以无论星期六晚玩到多晚，星期日还是会踊跃前往教堂做礼拜。圣公会圣约翰教堂是市内最大教堂，亦有循道公会、莫拉维亚会、天主教会、复临安息日会、浸信会、卫理公会、路德会、五旬节会等各个教堂，而一些较小规模的宗教团体，例如巴哈派教徒、穆斯林和印度教徒，都在此间和睦共处。

各个教会除了满足人们精神需要之外，在保存文化方面亦扮演着重要角色。例如，圣公会和莫拉维亚会所举办的食品节，便已成为全国性的活动，烹调厨艺跟各类展品和美食享用互相辉映。每逢这类活动，移民社群都能大显身手，日本料理寿司、多米尼加山鸡美食、蒙特塞拉特岛的焖炖嫩肉 (Montserratian kiddie stew)、以及来自基特达岛的一种强肾植物洋菝契食品，都纷纷出炉，叫人大快朵颐。同时，地道美食，例如泡腌米(血肠)布丁、海豚鲱鱼、用面粉、甜马铃薯及椰油制成的面团，以及煮鳕鱼等都非常受欢迎呢。

这些活动不单在于替教会进行筹募善款，亦实实在在表现着人们的自我肯定和重建信念；即是：尽管在来自北美的价值观念、有线电视及国际网络不断耳濡目染之下，我们在躯体上、在心底上，以及在灵性上，仍然是不折不扣的西印度群岛人。

安提瓜和巴布达 – 事实和数据

名称 ：安提瓜和巴布达

首都 ：圣约翰

面积和位置 ：安提瓜是英语通行的各个'背风群岛'(Leeward Islands) 中面积最大的海岛，长约 14 英哩 (23 公里)，阔 11 英哩(18 公里)，面积约为 108 平方英哩(280 平方公里)。最高点为 Boggy Peak，海拔 1319 英呎(402 米)。巴布达位于安提瓜以北约 30 英哩 (48 公里)，为一地形平坦的珊瑚岛，面积约为 68 平方英哩(176 平方公里)。

安提瓜和巴布达位于东加勒比海'背风群岛'(Leeward Islands) 中央，在赤道以北约北纬 17 度。南面为蒙特塞拉特岛和瓜德罗普岛，北面和西面为尼维斯岛、圣基特斯岛、圣巴特斯岛和圣马丁岛。

气候 ：气温由冬季月份华氏 70 多度(摄氏 21 度)，至夏天为 80 多度。年均降雨量只有 45 吋(114 厘米)，常年处于低湿度，是东加勒比海群岛中阳光最灿烂的地方。

国家元首 ：英国女王伊利莎白二世，总督詹姆斯.卡莱尔总督为代表。

总理 ：鲍德温.斯潘塞

人口 ： 69,481 (2007)

语言 ：英语

货币 ：东加勒比海元(EC$)； 美元 (US$) 亦接受

国际拨号 ： +1268

国际网络网域 ：ag

电力 ：岛上部分地区 110 伏特，其余地区 220 伏特。多数酒店两种电压通用。

银行 ： Antigua and Barbuda Development Bank, Antigua and Barbuda Investment Bank, Antigua Commercial Bank, Bank of Antigua, Bank of Nova Scotia, First Caribbean International Bank, Global Bank of Commerce, RBTT Bank, Royal Bank of Canada.

医疗设施 ：设有一间医院及一间私家诊疗所，并有多名全科医生及专科医生执业。岛上各地均有配药服务。

安提瓜和巴布达总督 James B. Carlisle (中间者)、副总理 Wilmoth Daniel、中国驻安提瓜和巴布达大使任小平在 Jolly Beach 渡假胜地庆祝中华人民共和国成立 55 周年。

护照和入境 ：美国、加拿大和欧盟国民须出示公民身份证明(有效护照或经认证出生证)。其它国家居民可联系他们就近的旅游办事处查询入境规定。

航空旅游

V.C. Bird International Airport 是旅客乘搭航班抵达安提瓜和巴布达的入境点。从北美洲经圣胡安及圣马丁均有直航及接驳航班开达，而欧洲亦每日有几个班次到达。设有定期及包机服务前往多个邻近海岛。

飞行时间：纽约 – 4 小时； 迈阿密 – 3 小时； 多伦多 – 4 小时；波多黎各 – 1 小时； 伦敦 – 8 小时； 法兰克福 – 9 小时； 巴黎 – 8 小时。

服务北美线航班 ： Air Canada、American Airlines、BWIA、Continental Airlines、US Air.

服务英国线航班 ： BWIA、British Airways、Virgin Atlantic 和 Sunsail Airways，均有接驳前往欧洲其它各地。

岛际航班 ：LIAT、 Air St Kitts/Nevis、Carib Aviation、Caribbean Star Airlines、Montserrat Airways、Caribbean Sun.

海上旅游

邮轮停泊码头位于圣约翰港及首都心脏地带的 Heritage Quay。

旅游办事处

美国

安提瓜和巴布达旅游及贸易部
Antigua and Barbuda Department of Tourism and Trade
25 S.E. 2nd Avenue, Suite 300, Miami, FL 33131

电话：305-381-6762
传真：305-381-7908
电邮：cganuear@bellsouth.net

安提瓜和巴布达旅游部
Antigua and Barbuda Department of Tourism
610 Fifth Avenue, Suite 311, New York, NY 10020

免费专线：888-268-4227
电话：212-541-4117
传真：212-541-4789
电邮：info@antigua-barbuda.org

安提瓜和巴布达大使馆
Embassy of Antigua and Barbuda
3216 New Mexico Avenue NW, Washington, DC 20016

电话：202 362 5122
传真：202 362 5225
电邮：embantbar@aol.com

加拿大

安提瓜和巴布达旅游及贸易部
Antigua and Barbuda Department of Tourism & Trade
60 St Claire Avenue East, Suite 304, Toronto, Ontario, M4T 1N5

电话：416-961-3085
传真：416-961-7218
电邮：info@antigua-barbuda-ca.com

英国

安提瓜和巴布达旅游办事处
Antigua and Barbuda Tourist Office
45 Crawford Place, London, W1H 4LP

电话：(44) 20 7258 0070
传真：(44) 20 7258 7486
网页：www.antigua-barbuda.com
电邮：antbar@msn.com

德国、奥地利、瑞士和北欧

安提瓜和巴布达旅游部
Fremdenverkehrsamt Antigua und Barbuda
Thomasstr. 11, D-61348 Bad Homburg, Germany

电话：49-6172-21504
传真：49-6172-21513

法国

安提瓜和巴布达旅游办事处
Office du Tourisme D'Antigua et Barbuda
43 Avenue de Friedland, Paris 75008

电话：33 (0) 1 53 75 15 71
传真 33 (0) 1 53 75 15 69

意大利

安提瓜和巴布达旅游部
Dipartimento del Turismo di Antigua e Barbuda
Via Santa Maria alla Porta, 9, 20123 Milan

电话/传真：(039) 02 877 983
电话（有关旅游业务）：(039) 02 720 987 27

安提瓜和巴布达

安提瓜和巴布达旅游部
Antigua and Barbuda Department of Tourism
Government Complex, Queen Elizabeth Highway, St John's

电话：268-462-0480
传真：268-462-2483
电邮：deptourism@antigua.gov.ag

安提瓜酒店及游客协会
Antigua Hotels & Tourists Association
Island House, New Gates Street, P.O. Box 454, St John's

电话：268-462-0374
传真：268-462-3702
电邮：ahta@candw.ag

GOVERNOR-GENERAL

H.E. Louise Agnetha Lake-Tack
Government House
Independence Avenue
St John's
Tel: 462-0003

MINISTERS OF GOVERNMENT

Hon. W. Baldwin Spencer
Prime Minister & Minister of Foreign Affairs
Tel: 462-0773

Hon. Justin L. Simon
Attorney General & Minister of Legal Affairs
Tel: 462-8867

Hon. Willmoth Daniel
Deputy Prime Minister & Minister of Works & Transportation
Tel: 462-0890

Dr Hon. L. Errol Cort
Minister of Finance & Economy
Tel: 462-3588

Hon. Harold E.E. Lovell
Minister of Tourism, Civil Aviation, Culture & Environment
Tel: 462-0787

Sen. Hon. Colin Derrick
Minister of Justice
Tel: 462-0017

Hon. Hilson Baptiste
Minister of Housing & Social Transformation
Tel: 562-5148

Dr Hon. Jacqui Quinn-Leandro
Minister of Labour, Public Administration & Empowerment
Tel: 562-3860

Hon. Bertrand Joseph
Minister of Education
Tel: 462-4959

Hon. John H. Maginley
Minister of Health
Tel: 562-1675

Hon. Charlesworth T. Samuel
Minister of Agriculture, Lands, Marine Resources & Agro Industries
Tel: 462-1007

Sen. Hon. Joanne Massiah
Minister of State attached to the Ministry of Agriculture, Lands, Marine Resources and Agro Industry with responsibility for Marine Affairs & Food Production
Tel: 562-4679

Hon. Trevor Walker
Minister of State attached to the Office of the Prime Minister with responsibility for Barbuda Affairs & Antigua Public Utilities Authority
Tel: 562-5029

Sen. Hon. Dr. Edmond Mansoor
Minister of State attached to the Office of the Prime Minister with responsibility for Information, Broadcasting & Telecommunications
Tel: 462-8899

Hon. Winston Williams
Minister of State attached to the Ministry of Education & Youth Affairs with responsibility for Youth Affairs
Tel: 462-5522

Hon. Eleston M. Adams
Minister of State attached to the Ministry of Tourism, Civil Aviation, Culture & Environment with responsibility for Culture including Independence, Community Pride & Homecoming Festivities
Tel: 462-0787

Sen. Hon. Lenworth Johnson
Parliamentary Secretary attached to the Ministry of Finance & Economy
Tel: 462-4860

HIGH COMMISSIONS, EMBASSIES & CONSULATES OF ANTIGUA AND BARBUDA OVERSEAS

CANADA
Consulate General of Antigua and Barbuda
60 St Clair Avenue East, Suite 601
Toronto, Ontario M4T 1N5
Tel: 416-961-3143. Fax: 416-961-7218

CUBA
Embassy of Antigua and Barbuda
9407 Crnr 66th & 5th Avenue, Miramar, Havana City
Tel: 537-207-9756. Fax: 537-207-9757
Email: haile.goodwin@gmail.com

PEOPLE'S REPUBLIC OF CHINA
Embassy of Antigua and Barbuda
Room No1N, Guomen Building No. 1, Zuojiazhuang, Chaoyang District, Beijing 100028
T: 86-106-460-6481. F: 86-106-460-6356

UNITED KINGDOM
High Commission for Antigua and Barbuda
2nd Floor, 45 Crawford Place
London W1H 4LP
T: 44-207-258-0070. F: 44-207-258-7486

UNITED STATES

Embassy of Antigua and Barbuda
3216 New Mexico Avenue, N.W.
Washington, DC 20016
Tel: 202-362-5122. Fax: 202-362-5225

Consulate General of Antigua and Barbuda
25 S.E. 2nd Avenue, Suite 300
Miami, FL 33131
Tel: 305-381-6762. Fax: 305-381-7908

Permanent Mission of Antigua & Barbuda to the United Nations
3 Dag Hammerskjöld Plaza
305 E. 47th Street, Room 6A
New York, NY 10017
Tel: 212-541-4117. Fax: 212-757-1607

TOURISM OFFICES OVERSEAS

CANADA
Antigua and Barbuda Department of Tourism and Trade
60 St Clair Avenue East, Suite 304,
Toronto, Ontario M4T 1N5
Tel: 416-961-3085
Fax: 416-961-7218
Email: info@antigua-barbuda-ca.com

FRANCE
Office du Tourisme D'Antigua and Barbuda
43 Avenue Freidland, Paris 75000
Tel: 053-75-15-71. Fax: 053-75-15-69
Email: ot.antigua-barbuda@wanadoo.fr

GERMANY, AUSTRIA, SWITZERLAND & NORTHERN EUROPE
Antigua and Barbuda Department of Tourism
Thomasstr.11, D61348 Bad Homburg, Germany
Tel: 49-6172-21504. Fax: 49-6172-21513
Email: antigua-barbuda@karibik.org

ITALY
Antigua and Barbuda Department of Tourism
Via S.Maria Alla Porta 9 20123, Milan
Tel: 03-92-87-79-83. Fax: 03-92-87-79-83
Email: infoantigua@antigua-barbuda.org

UNITED KINGDOM
Antigua and Barbuda Department of Tourism
2nd Floor, 45 Crawford Place
London W1H 4LP
T: 44-207-258-0070. F: 44-207-258-7486

UNITED STATES
Antigua and Barbuda Department of Tourism and Trade
25 S.E. 2nd Avenue, Suite 300
Miami, FL 33131
Tel: 305-381-6762
Fax: 305-381-7908
Email: cganuear@bellsouth.net

Antigua and Barbuda Department of Tourism and Trade
3 Dag Hammerskjöld Plaza
305 E. 47th Street, Room 6A
New York, NY 10017
Tel: 212-541-4117. Fax: 212-541-4789
Email: info@antigua-barbuda.org

EMERGENCY SERVICES

AMBULANCE   911
FIRE   911
POLICE   911 or 777

Ambulance
462-0251

Fire
462-0044

Police
462-0125

Air / Sea Rescue
462-3062

Alcoholics Anonymous (AA)
463-3155

Domestic Violence
463-5555

Friends Hotline
800-4357(HELP)

Hospital
462-0251

Office of Disaster Preparedness
462-4402

International dialling code for
Antigua and Barbuda: 1 268

AIR AMBULANCE SERVICES

AAA-Air Ambulance America
Tel: (800) 222-3564
Tel: (512) 479-8000

Aero Ambulance International
Tel: 461-8127

Aero Jet International
San Juan
Puerto Rico
Tel: (787) 724 1694
Fax: (787) 721 0721

Medical Air Services
Nevis Street
Tel: 462-6256
Fax: 463-9225

AIR CARGO SERVICES

Air Canada
V C Bird International Airport
Tel: 480-5730
Fax: 462-2679

American Airlines
V C Bird International Airport
Tel: 481-4675
Fax: 481-4660

Caribbean Airlines
V C Bird International Airport
Tel: 481-480-5725

LIAT
V C Bird International Airport
Tel: 480-5728 / 5736 / 5725
Fax: 480-5635

Virgin Atlantic
V C Bird International Airport
Tel: 480-5725
Fax: 562-1629

AIRCRAFT CHARTER RENTAL

Carib Aviation
V C Bird International Airport
Tel: 481-2400
Fax: 481-2405
Email: caribav@candw.ag

Caribbean Helicopters Ltd
Jolly Harbour
Tel: 460-5900
Fax: 460-5901

Norman Aviation Ltd
V C Bird International Airport
Tel: 462-2445. Fax: 462-2445

AIRLINE COMPANIES

Air Canada
V C Bird International Airport
Tel: 462-1147
Fax: 462-2679
Res & Info: 800-744-2472

Air Caribes Dca Ltd
V C Bird International Airport
Tel: 462-2523

American Airlines / American Eagle
V C Bird International Airport
Tel: 481-4651
Fax: 481-4660
Toll Free: 800-744-0006

BMI
V C Bird International Airport
Tel: 462-0528

British Airways
V C Bird International Airport
Tel: 462-0879. Fax: 462-3218

Carib Aviation
V C Bird International Airport
Tel: 481-2400
Fax: 481-2405
Email: caribav@candw.ag

Caribbean Airlines
Woods Centre
Tel: 480-2900
Fax: 480-2940
Res & Flight info: 800-538-2942

Continental Airlines
V C Bird International Airport
Tel: 462-5355

LIAT (1974) Ltd
V C Bird International Airport
Tel: 480-5600
Fax: 480-5635

US Airways
Tel: (800) 622-1015

Virgin Atlantic
V C Bird International Airport
Tel: 560-2079
Fax: 562-1629
Res & Flight info: 800-744-7477

AIRLINE & AIRCRAFT SUPPORT SERVICES

Airport Services (Antigua) Ltd ASA
V C Bird International Airport
Tel: 462-0528
Fax: 462-8999
Email: asa@candw.ag

Bizjet-to-Yacht Antigua Ltd
V C Bird International Airport
Tel: 562-4347
Fax: 562-1689

Carib Aviation
V C Bird International Airport
Tel: 481-2400
Fax: 481-2405
Email: caribav@candw.ag

FBO 2000 Antigua Ltd
V C Bird International Airport
Runway 10
Tel: 462-2522
Fax 462-5185

AIRPORT

V C Bird International Airport
Main Office: 462-3082
Air Traffic Control: 562-0302
Fire Station: 462-3062 / 63
Security Division: 462-4670
Meteorological Services: 462-0930
VIP Lounge: 462-4605

APARTMENTS & CONDOMINIUM RENTALS & SALES

Amor Villas
Crosbies
Tel: 481-6602
Fax: 481-6606

Antigua Village Condominium
Beach Resort
Dickenson Bay
Tel: 462-2930
Fax: 462-0375

Barrymore Beach Club
Runaway Beach
Tel: 462-4101. Fax: 462-4140

Barrymore Properties
Runaway Bay
Tel: 462-4102

Benjies Villas
Crawl Bay
Tel: 460-4474

Brown's Bay Villas
Browns Bay
Tel: 460-4173. Fax: 460-4175

Coolidge Apartments
Atlantic Avenue
Tel: 460-2914

Coral Sands
Runaway Bay
Tel: 461-0925

Coral Villas
Crosbies
Tel: 461-3278. Fax: 461-3278

Crabbs Cabanas
Crabbs Peninsular
Tel: 461-2113. Fax: 463-3750

Eden Place Apartments / SE Realty
All Saints Road
Tel: 560-4451. Fax: 560-4451

Emerald Cove Ltd.
Nonsuch Bay
Tel: 463-2391. Fax: 463-2373

Fountain Hill Village
Marble Hill
Tel: 461-3239

Gefino's Apartments
Old Parham Road
Tel: 462-1746. Fax: 462-7206

Hadeed S&E Apartments
Crosbies
Tel: 462-0877. Fax: 462-4674

Harbour View Apartments
Falmouth
Tel: 460-1762

Marble Hill Apartments
Marble Hill
Tel: 461-5557

Maxi Apartments
Factory Road
Tel: 462-2282

Nedds Guest House
Barbuda
Tel: 460-0059

O'Beez Apartments
Factory Road
Tel: 461-4661. Fax: 462-5363

Runaway Beach Club
Runaway
Tel: 462-1318. Fax: 462-4172

Sea Fern Apartments
Hodges Bay
Tel: 560 6242

South Coast Horizons
Cades Bay
Tel: 460-7915. Fax: 463-3177

Time-A-Way Apartments
Runaway Bay
Tel: 462-0775. Fax: 462-2587

Vacation Villas Antigua
Runaway Beach
Tel: 462-4101

Whitegate Cottages & Apartments
Campsite
Tel: 462-1285. Fax: 462-0900

ART GALLERIES & MUSEUMS

2000 Millennium Art Gallery & Gift
Shop
Jolly Harbour
Tel: 562-3987

Afrikcarib
Heritage Quay
Tel: 562-0280

The Art Gallery
Jolly Harbour
Tel: 562-3987

Calypso Graphics / Gilly Gobinet
Runaway Bay
Tel: 461-0761. Fax: 461-0761

Dockyard Museum
Nelson's Dockyard
Tel: 460-8181

Gomac Art Gallery
St Mary's Street
Tel: 460-7245

Harmony Hall
Brown's Bay Mill
Tel: 460-4120

Hide Restaurant & Art Gallery
Mamora Bay
Tel: 460-3666. Fax: 460-3667

Island Arts & The Yoda Guy
Heritage Quay
Tel: 462-2787
Fax: 462-1480

Kate Design
Redcliffe Quay
Tel: 460-5971
Fax: 460-5972 / 3

Museum of Antigua & Barbuda
Long Street
Tel: 462-1469 / 462-4930

Real Local Art Gallery
Falmouth Main Road
Tel: 562-5159

Rhythm of Blue Art Gallery
Dockyard Drive
Tel: 562-2230

Woods Gallery
Woods Mall
Tel: 462-2332

AUTOMOBILE DEALERS

Ace Enterprises Ltd
Tomlinson's
Tel: 462-1289
Fax: 462-1290
Email: harneymo@candw.ag

Antigua Motors (1993) Ltd
Old Parham Road
Tel: 462-3234
Fax: 462-0395

Cars.com
Factory Road.
Tel: 562-2277
Fax: 562-2277

Hadeed Motors
Old Parham Road
Tel: 481-2500
Fax: 481-2525
Email: hadeedmotors@yahoo.com

Harney Motors Ltd
Factory & American Roads
Tel: 462-1062
Fax: 462-1024
Email: harneymo@candw.ag

Ideal Autos Ltd
Cassada Gardens
Tel: 481-3590
Fax: 481-3591

Island Motors Ltd
Queen Elizabeth Highway
Tel: 462-2199
Fax: 462-2138

Prestige Motors ltd
American Road
Tel: 481-7695. Fax: 481-7696

Shaw Brothers Enterprises
Fort Road
Tel: 462-4981. Fax: 462-4981

AUTOMOBILE RENTALS

ATS Car Rental & Limousine
Service
Powell's Estate
Tel: 562-1709
Fax: 461-5700
Email: atslimousine@yahoo.com

Avis Rent-A-Car
Powell's Estate
Tel: 462-2840
Fax: 462-2848
Email: avisanu@candw.ag

Bigs Car rental & Taxi Service
English Harbour
Tel: 562-4901

Budget Rent-a-Car
Cassada Gardens
Tel: 462-3009
Fax: 460-9177

Capital Car Rentals
Gambles Terrace
Tel: 463-0675

Carters Rent-a-Car
V C Bird International Airport
Tel: 463-0675

Coleds Car Rental & Leasing
Gambles Terrace
Tel: 526-4597
Fax: 462-0464
Email: coleds@hotmail.com

Dions Rent-a-Car & Tax Service
V C Bird International Airport
Tel: 462-3466
Fax: 461-3267

Dollar Rent-a-Car
Factory Road
Tel: 462-0362
Fax: 462-5907
Email: dollar@candw.ag

Europcar
Airport Road.
Tel: 562-2708. Fax: 562-2707

Hertz Rent-a-Car
Carlisle Estate
Tel: 481-4440. Fax: 481-4460
Email: hertzag@candw.ag

Huntley Car Rental
Alfred Peters Street
Tel: 462-1575

Ivor's Taxi
Liberta Village
Tel: 460-1241

Jacobs Rent-a-Car
V C Bird International Airport
Tel: 462-0576

Jeeps 'r' Us Rentals
Tindale Road
Tel: 462-9099

Jonas Rent-a-Car
Factory Road
Tel: 462-3760. Fax: 463-7625

Koconut Rent-a-Car
Buckley's Village
Tel: 460-2407

Lions Car Rental
Airport Road
Tel: 460-1400
Fax: 562-2707

National Car Rental
Fax: 462-2113

Oakland Rent-a-Car
V C Bird International Airport
Tel: 462-3021
Fax: 560-1232

Paradise Car Rental
Rex Halcyon Cove
Tel: 462-9780

Pats Rent-a-Car
Crosbies
Tel: 462-6739

Prince's Rent-a-Car
Fort Road
Tel: 462-0766

Rawlins Supreme Car Rental
St Johnston's Village
Tel: 461-0110
Fax: 461-1878

Richards Rent-a-Car
V C Bird International Airport
Tel: 462-0976

St John's Car Rental
Branch Avenue
Tel: 462-0594. Fax: 462-6147

Slane's Supreme Car
Lower Newgate Street
Tel: 462-8789

Sted Rent-a-Car
Airport Road
Tel: 462-9970
Fax: 460-5603

Thrifty Car Rental
V C Bird International Airport
Tel: 462-0976
Fax: 463-9030

TiTi Rent-a-car
English Harbour
Tel: 460-1452

Tropical Rentals
Tel: 562-5180

Village Car Rental
Anchorage Road
Tel: 461-3746

BANKS

Antigua & Barbuda Development
Bank
St Mary's Street
St John's
Tel: 462-0838
Fax: 462-0839

Antigua & Barbuda Investment
Bank Ltd
Redcliffe Street
St John's
Tel: 480-2700
Fax: 480-2850
Email: abib@abifinancial.com

Antigua Commercial Bank
St Mary's Street
St John's
Tel: 481-4200
Fax: 481-4280

Antigua Overseas Bank Ltd
Redcliffe Street, St John's
Tel: 480-2700
Fax: 480-2750
Email: aob@abifinancial.com

Bank of Antigua Ltd
Airport Boulevard
Tel: 480-5300
Fax: 480-5433

Barrington Bank
Woods Centre
St John's
Tel: 481-1777. Fax: 481-1778
Email: common@barrington.ag

Caribbean Union Bank
Friars Hill Road
Tel: 481-8278

East Caribbean Central Bank
Factory Road, St John's
Tel: 462-2489
Fax: 462-2490

First Caribbean International Bank
Ltd
High Street
St John's
Tel: 480-5000
Fax: 462-4910

Global Bank of Commerce
Woods Centre
St John's
Tel: 480-2240
Fax: 462-1831
Email: customer.service@gbc.ag

PKB Privatbank Ltd
10 Redcliffe Quay
Tel: 481-1250
Fax: 481-1263

RBTT Bank Ltd
High Street
St John's
Tel: 481-7288
Fax: 462-5040

Royal Bank of Canada
High & Market Streets
St John's
Tel: 480-1150. Fax: 480-1190

Scotiabank
High Street
St John's
Tel: 480-1500
Fax: 480-1554

Stanford International Bank Ltd
Pavilion Drive
Coolidge
Tel: 480-3700
Fax: 480-3737
Email: sibprivate@stanfordeagle.com

BARS

Daddy Boy Bar
Nevis Street
Tel: 462-9658

Darkwood Beach Bar
Johnsons Point
Tel: 462-8240

George Restaurant & Bar
Market & Redcliffe Streets
Tel: 562-4866

Spliff Bar & Grill
Old Parham Road
Tel: 562-5138

Turners Beach Bar & Grill
Johnsons point
Tel: 462-9133

BEAUTY SALONS

Akparo
Nelson's Dockyard
Tel: 460-5705

Beauty Box
Newgate Street
Tel: 462-5963

Beauty Vibes
Cross Street
Tel: 460-8648

Brantilla's Touch of Beauty
Tanner Street
Tel: 562-4024

Cicely's Beauty Salon
Lionel Hurst Street
Tel: 462-1836

The Cutting Edge
Jasmine Court
Friar's Hill Road
Tel: 562-1415

D'Elegance Beauty Salon
Cnr All Saints & Bendals Roads
Tel: 562-6298

Dionne's Unisex Hair Gallery
Cassada Gardens
Tel: 461-5778

Glenette's Beauty salon
Newgate Street
Tel: 462-1030

Gloria's Beauty Salon
Cross Street
Tel: 462-1325

Hair in Action
Fort Road & Rowan Henry Street
Tel: 462-1235

Hollywood Best Look Barber Shop &
Beauty Salon
South Street
Tel: 462-2378

L.A. Hair.com
Old Parham Road
Tel: 461-4247

Mingles Unisex Salon & Day Spa
Cross & Nevis Streets
Tel: 461-9696

Vanity Beauty Salon
Deanery Lane
Tel: 462-0970

BEAUTY THERAPY & MASSAGE

Akparo
Nelson's Dockyard
Tel: 460-5705

Alternative Body Care
Redcliffe Quay
Tel: 460-8748

Chakra Body Works
Jolly Harbour
Tel: 560-3326

Equilibrium
Marble Hill
Tel: 560-3780

Equilibrium Health Spa
Gambles Medical Centre
Friars Hill Road
Tel: 462-7919

Christine Gillis-Gerrad
Physiotherapist
c/o Equilibrium
Marble Hill
Tel: 560-3780

BEER & WINE RETAILERS (SEE LIQUOR, BEER & WINE RETAILERS)

BOAT DEALERS

Leeward Islands Boat Sales
Shell Beach
Tel: 562-3499. Fax: 562-3499

Paradise Boat Sales
Old Parham Road
Tel: 562-7125
Fax: 462-6276
Email: paradise@candw.ag

BOAT RENTAL & CHARTER

Antigua Charter Services
Nelson's Dockyard
Tel: 460-2615
Fax: 460-2616

Brief Encounter Tours
Dickenson Bay
Tel: 463-4653

Caribbean Development Antigua Ltd
Jolly Harbour
Tel: 462-7686

Caribbean Water Sport Sail
Tel: 462-7245

Cay Heaven Charters
All Saints
Tel: 462-0834

Coral Ark Love Boat
Redcliffe Street
Tel: 462-9731

Creole Cruises Ltd.
Jolly Harbour
Tel: 460-5130
Fax: 561-3894
Email: creolecruises@candw.ag

Excellence / Tiami
Redcliffe Street
St John's
Tel: 480-1225. Fax: 462-2065
Email: tropad@candw.ag

Kokomo Cat Cruises
Jolly Harbour
Tel: 462-7245
Fax: 462-8305

Miguel's Holiday Adventure
Villa
Tel: 461-0361

Paradise Boat Sales
Old Parham Road
Tel: 562-7125. Fax: 462-6276
Email: paradise@candw.ag

Sea Spa Private Charters
Jolly Harbour
Tel: 726-1009

Sunsail
Nelson's Dockyard
Tel: 463-6224
Fax: 460-2616
Email: charterservices@candw.ag

Sun Yacht Charters
Nelson's Dockyard
Tel: 460-2615. Fax: 460-2616

Treasure Island Cruises
Five Islands
Tel: 461-8675. Fax: 461-8698
Email: armstronge@candw.ag

Wadadli Cats
Redcliffe Quay
Tel: 462-4792. Fax: 462-3661

BOAT BUILDERS

Woodstock Boatbuilders
Dockyard Drive
English Harbour
Tel: 463-6359. Fax: 562-6359

BOAT REPAIRS

A-1 Marine Service
Jolly Harbour
Tel: 462-7755

A&F Sails Ltd
Nelson's Dockyard
Tel: 460-1522. Fax 460-1152
Email: afsails@candw.ag

Antigua Marine Services
Shell Beach
Tel: 562-3499

Harris Boat Works Co. Ltd
Jolly Harbour Marina
Tel: 462-5333
Fax: 562-5970

Leeward Islands Boat Sales
Shell Beach
Tel: 562-3499
Fax: 562-3499
Email: ams@candw.ag

BOAT YARDS

Antigua Slipway
English Harbour
Tel: 460-1056

Antigua Yacht Club Marina
Falmouth Harbour
Tel: 460-1544

Bailey's Boatyard
Falmouth
Tel: 460-1036

Falmouth Harbour Marina
Tel: 460-6054
Fax: 460-6055
Email: falmar@candw.ag

Jolly Harbour Marina
Jolly Harbour
Tel: 462-6042. Fax: 462-7703

Nelson's Dockyard Marina
Nelson's Dockyard
Tel: 460-7976 / 1379 / 1380

Shell Beach Marina
Shell Beach
Tel: 562-0185

BOOKSELLERS & NEWSAGENTS

Adventist Book Centre
Nevis Street
Tel: 462 4546

Best of Books
St Mary's Street
St John's
Tel: 562 3198
Fax: 562 3198
Email: bestofbooks@yahoo.com

Caribbean Educational Services Ltd
St Mary's Street
St John's
Tel: 462 3993. Fax: 462 3995

Christian Bookshop
Newgate Lane, St John's
Tel: 463 5474. Fax: 463 5474

Christian Literature Centre
Lower Church Street
St John's
Tel: 462 2024
Fax: 462 2023

Frame-it (1991) Ltd
St Mary's Street
St John's
Tel: 462 3993
Fax: 462 3995

G&L Bookshop
St Mary's Street
St John's
Tel: 460 5504
Fax: 462 1884

Island Newstand
Bob Camacho's Arcade
Lower High Street
St John's
Tel: 462 2457
Fax: 462 2458

Lord Jim's Locker
Antigua Yacht Club Marina
English Harbour
Tel: 460 1147
Fax: 560 4093

Map Shop
St Mary's Street
St John's
Tel: 462 3993
Fax: 462 3995

Methodist Book Shop
Upper St Mary's Street
Tel: 462-3864
Fax: 461-1424

PC's Book Review
Corner of St Mary's Street
St John's
Tel: 462 1545

Seventh Day Adventist Book Centre
Tanner Street, St John's
Tel: 462 4546

Stermat Bookstore
1b Newgate Lane
St John's
Tel: 462 0018
Fax: 462 1058

BRIDAL SHOPS

Annlins Bridal & Tuxedo
Cnr Church Street & Corn Alley
Tel: 773-3354

E & G Bridal
Potters Main Road
Tel: 462-4002
Fax: 462-5344

CASINOS

Asot's Arcade Jackpot Casino
Patrick Michael Building
High Street
Tel: 462-2359

Gold Coin Arcade
Corn Alley
Tel: 462-2077

Grand Princess Entertainment
Complex
Jolly Harbour
Tel: 562-9900

Joe Mike's Hotel Plaza
Nevis Street
Tel: 462-1142
Fax: 462-6056

Keno's Palace
St Mary's Street
Tel: 460-7777

King's Casino
Heritage Quay
Tel: 462-1727
Fax: 462-1724

Madison Casino
Runaway Bay
Tel: 562-7874

CELLULAR TELEPHONES

Cable & Wireless (WI) Ltd
Tel: 480-4000

Digicel
Woods Mall & Redcliffe Street
Tel: 480-2050 / 481-3444

PCS Mobile Service
Long Street
Tel: 727-2782

CHEMISTS (SEE PHARMACIES)

CHIROPRACTORS

Allred Chiropractors Clinic
43 Upper Redcliffe Street
St John's
Tel: 462-3266

CINEMAS

Deluxe Theatre Ltd
High Street St John's
Tel: 462-2188
Fax: 462-6259

CLINICS

Adolescent Clinic
Factory Road
Tel: 462-8850

St John's Health Centre
Lower All Saints Road
Tel: 462-1891

All Saints: 460-1003
Bendals: 462-3841
Bethesda: 463-2805
Bolans: 462-3606
Cedar Grove: 462-1011
Clare Hall: 462-4127
Cobbs Cross: 460-3400
Freetown: 462-5365
Grays Farm: 462-0681
Jennings: 462-6304
Judges Hill: 462-3114
Liberta: 460-3175
Newfield: 460-4270
Old Road: 462-8255
Ottos New Town: 462-1623
Pares: 463-2622
Parham: 463-2576
Pigotts: 462-1271
Potters: 462-4692
Swetes: 460-1174
Willikies: 460-9350

COMPANY FORMATION

Richards & Company
The Colony House
41 Nevis Street
St John's
Tel: 562-1705
Fax: 562-1706
Email: Richards@candw.ag

Ward Associates
11 Old Parham Road
Tel: 462-6355
Fax: 462-6354

COMPUTER DEALERS

ACT Antigua Technology Co Ltd
Market & Church Streets
St John's
Tel: 480-5228
Fax: 480-5226

Comnett Ltd
Redcliffe Quay
St John's
Tel: 462-1040. Fax: 562-8324

Computer Reset
Old Parham Road
Tel: 560-3867

Cyber Centre
Newgate Street
St John's
Tel: 462-2638
Fax: 462-2658

Illuminat
St Mary's Street
St John's
Tel: 481-1101
Fax: 481-1144
Email:
illuminate.ag@illuminatnm.com

Internet Connections
Upper High Street
Tel: 480-3000. Fax: 480-3003

Microcom Ltd
Aflak Building
Friars Hill Road
Tel: 462-2891. Fax: 462-3507

Napka Systems
Old Parham Road
Tel: 562-5455. Fax: 562-5456

CONSTRUCTION COMPANIES

3-D Engineering & Construction
Airport Road
Tel: 562-8453. Fax: 462-4953

Antigua Public Utilities Authority
St John's
Tel: 480-7000
Email: apuaops@candw.ag

ATH Construction
English Harbour
Tel: 560-6332. Fax: 560-6332

Caribbean Concrete Ltd
St John's
Tel: 764-3115. Fax: 562-5378

Civil Engineering & Associated
Services Ltd
St John's
Tel: 764-2327
Fax: 562-2327

G-90 Building Systems Ltd
St John's
Tel: 481-4601
Fax: 481-4619

Henderson (2004) Ltd
Coolidge Industrial Estate, St John's
Tel: 481-7663
Fax: 481-7660

Khouly Construction & Engineering
Ltd
Long Street, St John's
Tel: 480-9055
Fax: 480-9035
Email: khouly@actol.net

Modern Image Construction Co Ltd
St Mary's
Tel: 562-6422
Fax: 562-6423

S.U.S. Construction Ltd
St John's
Tel: 562-2941
Fax: 562-2942

Vega Development Inc
St John's
Tel: 562-4656

Willy D Enterprises
All Saints Road, St John's
Tel: 462-9609
Fax: 462-9609

Wyndham Construction
St John's
Tel: 562-1518
Fax: 560-2756

CONSULATES, EMBASSIES & FOREIGN GOVERNMENT REPRESENTATIVES

Consulate for Austria
c/o Yepton Hotel
P.O. Box 1448
Tel: 462-2520. Fax: 462-3240

Consulate for Barbados
P.O. Box 585
St John's
Tel: 462-3122. Fax: 462-3479

Consulate for Colombia
P.O. Box 734
St John's
Tel: 560-4622
Fax: 481-4126
Email: luan@hotmail.com

Consulate for Denmark
Upstairs Harpers Building
P.O. Box 104
High Street
Tel: 480-3070
Fax: 480-3076
Email: hallm@candw.ag

Consulate for France
P.O. Box Woods 211
Tel: 460-6428
Fax: 462-6686

Consulate for the Federal Republic
of Germany
P.O. Box 1259
Hodges Bay
Tel: 462-3174
Fax: 462-3496

Consulate for Guyana
c/o Sun Images
1st Avenue Gambles Terrace
Tel: 462-4320 / 562-5314
Fax: 462-4320 / 462-6441

Consulate for Italy
Antigua Yacht Club Marina
Falmouth
Tel: 460-1543
Fax: 460-1444

Consulate for Jamaica
6 Temple Street
P.O. Box 2372
Tel: 460-6184
Fax: 460-6183

Consulate for The Netherlands
c/o Kenneth A. Gomez & Sons
High Street
P.O. Box 195
Tel: 462-0308
Fax: 462-2472
Email: kagomez@candw.ag

Consulate for Norway
c/o Francis Trading Enterprises
High Street
Tel: 462-4555
Fax: 462-0849

Consulate for Portugal
c/o Antigua Distillery
Friar's Hill Road
P.O. Box 149
Tel: 480-3202
Fax: 480-3215

Consulate for Spain
P.O. Box 15
7 St George's Street
Tel: 462-0889. Fax: 462-1651

Consulate for Switzerland
Swiss Consular Agency
Woods Centre
Friar's Hill Road
Tel: 462-8975 / 562-1122
Fax: 462-1262

Consular Agency for the United
States
Jasmin Court
Friar's Hill Road
Tel: 463-6531
Fax: 460-1569

High Commission for Britain
Old Parham Road
St John's
Tel: 462-0008
Fax: 562-2124

Embassy of the Republic of Cuba
Longfords Main Road
St John's
Tel: 562-5864
Fax: 562-5865

Embassy of the People's Republic
of China
P.O. Box 1446
St John's
Tel: 462-1125 / 462-6414
Fax: 462-6425

Embassy of Venezuela
Jasmine Court
Friar's Hill Road
P.O. Box 1201
Tel: 462-1574 / 462-8923
Fax: 462-1570

COURIER SERVICES

Caribbean Star Airlines
Airport Road
Tel: 480-2500
Email:
starpac@flycaribbeanstar.com

LIAT Quikpak
Cargo Terminal
V.C. Bird Int'l Airport
Tel: 480-5728
Fax: 480-5853
Email: quikpak@liatairline.com

Mail Boxes Etc.
Old Parham Road
Tel: 562-5090. Fax: 562-5089

Unlimited Services Plus
14 Redcliffe Quay
Tel: 562-7587. Fax: 462-4854

Wings Courier
High & Temple Streets
Tel: 460-3660. Fax: 460-3662

Xpress Courier
M & M Avenue
Old Parham Road
Tel: 462-1197. Fax: 560-9647

CUSTOMS

Customs Department
Main Office, St John's
Tel: 462-0026. Fax: 462-2767

Barbuda: 460-0085
Coolidge Cargo: 462-3160
Crabbs: 463-2372
Deep Water Harbour: 462-0814
Departure Tax: 562-4394
Dockyard: 460-1397
Heritage Quay: 462-6656
Jolly Harbour: 462-7929
Redcliffe Quay: 562-1577
V C Bird International Baggage:
462-3092

CUSTOMS BROKERS

Brysons Shipping Agency
Long Street
Tel: 480-1240
Fax: 462-0170

Coleds Brokerage Services Ltd
1st Avenue Gambles Terrace
Tel: 562-4597
Fax: 462-0464

F&G Trading
Lwr Dickenson Bay Street
Tel: 561-1831
Fax: 561-1832

Francis Trading Agency Ltd
High Street
Tel: 462-0854
Fax: 462-0849
Email: ftabrok@candw.ag

Henry's Customs Brokerage &
Shipping Services
North Street
Tel: 462-1390

Inter-Freight Ltd
Lwr Bishopgate Street
Tel: 481-1200
Fax: 481-1209

S&B Brokerage
Long Street
Tel: 462-4958. Fax: 462-4781

Vernon G. Edwards
Cnr Thames & Long Streets
Tel: 462-2034
Fax: 462-2035

Walker's Trading Agency
North Street
Tel: 462-4121
Fax: 462-4122

Wings Brokerage
High & Temple Streets
Tel: 460-3660. Fax: 460-3662

DENTISTS

A A-Antigua Barbuda Dental Group
Newgate Street
St Jon's
Tel: 460-3368
Fax: 462-2777

Dr Bernard Evan-Wong
Gambles Medical Centre
Tel: 462-3050
Fax: 463-9601

Family Dentistry
Cross & Newgate Streets
St John's
Tel: 462-0058
Fax: 462-2777

Dr Maxwell Francis
Cross & Newgate Streets
St John's
Tel: 462-0058
Fax: 462-2777

Gentle Dental Services
High Street
Tel: 462-2000
Fax: 460-7276

Ghanem Suetiana Dental Clinic
Redcliffe Street
St John's
Tel: 562-5393

Dr Jamil Hadeed
Lower All Saints Road
Tel: 462-2820

Island Smiles Dentistry
Deanery Lane
Tel: 562-6073
Fax: 562-6073

Jammula & Associates Dental
Practice
Upstairs Nature's Family Store
Tel: 562-4972
Cell: 464-3728

Dr Derek Marshall & Associates
Ramco Building
Tel: 462-2525
Fax: 462-2553

Dr S V Raj
Bishop Lodge Building
Tel: 461-6810
Fax: 461-6810

Dr Sengupta & Associates
Woods Centre
Tel: 462-9312
Fax: 462-9314

Seventh Day Adventist Dental Clinic
Nevis Street
Tel: 462-9393
Fax: 462-9633

Dr B K Wassouf
Family Dentist
Dollar Building
Tel: 462-9443

Williams & Associates Dental Clinic
28 Long Street
Tel: 462-1381
Fax: 460-6300

DEPARTMENT STORES

Antigua Home & Garden Discount
Centre
Old Parham Road
Tel: 562-0268. Fax: 562-0219

Antigua Home & Office Depot
Old Parham Road
Tel: 462-2403
Fax: 480-2390

Big Deal Dollar Store & More
Scotts Hill
Tel: 460-7400
Fax: 460-7401

Shoul's Chief Store
Market & St Mary's Streets
Tel: 462-1160
Fax: 462-1139

Shoul's Toys Gifts & Housewares
Newgate Street
Tel: 462-4357
Fax: 462-1788

Sight, Sound & Time Gift Shop
Newgate Street
Tel: 462-5702
Fax: 462-1006

DIVING & SNORKELLING

AquaSports
Jolly Harbour
Tel: 480-3095
Fax: 480-3091

Dockyard Divers
Nelson's Dockyard
English Harbour
Tel: 460-1178
Fax: 460-5850

Jolly Dive Antigua
Jolly Harbour
Tel: 462-8305
Fax: 4628305

Ultra Marine
Tel: 463-DIVE / 3483
Fax: 560-5062
Cell: 720-9993
Email: enquries@ultramarine.com

DIVING EQUIPMENT
SUPPLIERS

AquaSports
55B Heritage Quay
Tel: 480-3090
Fax: 480-3091

DOCTORS

Dr Dane Abbott – Obstetrician /
Gynaecologist
Women's Clinic
Tel: 462-4133
Fax: 462-4134

Antigua Optical Co Ltd
Stapleton Lane Clinic
Tel: 462-0031
Fax: 462-0031

Dr Jason Belizaire
Internal Medicine
Woods Centre
Tel: 562-1168. Fax: 562-1200

Dr Philmore Benjamin
Vivian Richards Street
Tel: 462-3630. Fax: 462-3630

Dr Jillia Bird – Optometrist
Milburn House
Tel: 462-1513
Fax: 462-5622

Dr Salah Bittar
Lower Nevis Street
Tel: 462-1706
Fax: 462-1706

Dr Carrick-Fraser
Alpha Building
Tel: 462-1975
Fax: 460-5258

Dr Kelvin P. Charles
Long Street
Tel: 462-4973

Dr Delrose Christian
Market & Tanner Streets
Tel: 462-5752
Fax: 462-5752

Dr Ronnie Cooper – Visiting
Dermatologist
Ramco Building
Tel: 462-6241
Email: ronniecooper@hotmail.com

Dr Raymond Daoud
St John's Street
Tel: 462-6149. Fax: 460-8584

Dr Alvin Edwards
Upper Redcliffe Street
St John's
Tel: 462-2748
Fax: 462-1976

Dr Gwendolyn Fevrier-Roberts –
Obstetrician / Gynecologist
Ramco Building
Tel: 462-2770. Fax: 462-1805

Dr Nicholas Fuller
Long Street
Tel: 462-0391

Dr Leroy Gardner
Caribbean Life-Style Health Centre
50 Upper Church Street
Tel: 463-5726

Dr Edda Hadeed – Pediatrician &
Neonatologist
Gambles Medical Centre
Tel: 462-9499
Fax: 461-4282

Dr Elijah James
Newfield Village
Tel: 562-1885. Fax: 562-1884

Dr Joseph John – Surgeon
Medical Surgical Associates
Tel: 562-1169
Fax: 562-3300

Dr Marlene Joseph – Family
Physician
Independence Drive
Tel: 462-0542

Dr Frances Kelsick – Obstetrician /
Gynecologist
Women's Clinic
Tel: 462-4133
Fax: 462-4134

Dr Sam Kiwomya
Temple & Tanner Street
Tel: 462-2990

Dr Linda Lovell-Roberts –
Paediatrician
2nd Avenue Gambles
Tel: 462-3710. Fax: 462-3105

Dr Edmond Mansoor
Market & Tanner Streets
Tel: 462-4634
Fax: 462-2633

Dr Rose Massiah – Family
Physician
41 Church Street
Tel: 562-2833. Fax: 562-2784

Dr Fouad Naffouj
Dollar Building
Tel: 562-1620
Fax: 462-9443

Dr Bertrand O'Marde – Surgeon
Ramco Building
Tel: 462-1935
Fax: 462-1835

Ortho Medical Associates
Woods Centre
St John's
Tel: 460-7720
Fax: 461-8065

Dr P Raj
Ramco Building
Tel: 462-6241

Dr George Roberts – ENT, Head &
Neck Surgeon
Ramco Building
Tel: 462-2770
Fax: 462-1805

Dr Raymond Rogers
Stapleton Lane Clinic
Tel: 462-0031
Fax: 462-0031

Dr Soumitra SenGupta
Temple Street
Tel: 462-1467

Dr K K Singh – Orthopaedic
Surgeon
Ortho Medical Associates
Woods Centre
Tel: 462-1932. Fax: 461-8065

Dr Nidhi Singh – Family Physician
(Specialist in Addiction)
Ortho Medical Associates
Woods Centre
St John's
Tel: 460-7720
Fax: 461-8065

Dr Arlene Sorhaindo – Pediatrician
Stapleton Lane
Tel: 562-1931
Fax: 562-1931

Dr Ian C Walwyn – Ophthalmologist
Stapleton Lane
Tel: 562-1931
Fax: 562-1931

Dr R A Walwyn – Ophthalmologist
Tel: 462-0031
Fax: 462-0031

Dr Andre Winter – Obstetrician /
Gynecologist
Tel: 562-1977
Fax: 562-1978

DUTY FREE RETAIL –
HERITAGE QUAY MALL

Abbott's Jewellery & Perfumery
Tel: 462-3108

Athlete's Foot
Tel: 462-9772

Beach Stuff
Tel: 462-3610

Benetton
Tel: 462-3273

The Body Shop
Tel: 462-4779

The Camera Shop
Tel: 462-3619

Caribbean Gems
Tel: 462-3670

Colombian Emeralds International
Tel: 462-3462 / 462-2343
Fax: 462-3463

Diamonds International
Tel: 481-1880

The Edge
Tel: 562-3343

Gingerlily
Tel: 462-3168

Heritage Sports
Tel: 462-2809

Island Arts & The Yoda Guy
Tel: 462-2787

Jeweller's Warehouse
Tel: 462-2343

Linen Shop
Tel: 462-3611

Lipstick
Tel: 562-1130 / 1133

Longchamp
Tel: 562-5301

Mimosa
Tel: 462-2923

The Music Shop
Tel: 460-6858

Passions
Tel: 562-5295

Quinn Farara's Liquor Store
Tel: 462-1737

Shipwreck
Tel: 562-4625

Sterlings
Tel: 562-5662

Sunseakers
Tel: 462-4523

Tanzanite International
Tel: 481-1880

Tropic Wear
Tel: 462-6251

DUTY FREE RETAIL – REDCLIFFE QUAY

Exotic Antigua
Tel: 562-1288

Jacaranda
Tel: 462-1888

Nature's Eyes
Tel: 562-1322

New Gates
Tel: 562-1627

FERRY SERVICES

Barbuda Express Ltd
P.O. Box 1816
Tel: 560-7989 / 764-2291
Website: www.antiguaferries.com

FINANCE COMPANIES

Finance & Development Co Ltd
Old Parham Road
Tel: 481-2569. Fax: 481-2571

Financial Services Corp
Tel: 463-2265
Fax: 462-3330

Stanford Financial Group Ltd
Tel: 480-5900
Fax: 480-5909

FITNESS CENTRES

Antigua Athletic Club
No. 24 Pavilion Drive
Tel: 480-6600

Impak Fitness Centre
All Saints Village
Tel: 764-3402

National Fitness Centre
Campsite
Tel: 462-3681

Paradise Fitness
Upper North Street
Tel: 562-2950

Valley Creek Fitness Centre
Valley Road
Tel: 722-0310

FLORISTS

Annette's Orchids
Paradise View Drive
Tel: 461-9496

Bailey's Countryside Flowers
Falmouth
Tel: 460-2200

Exotic Flowers
Thames Street
Tel: 728-0792

Flamboyant Flower Shop
Briggins Road
Tel: 462-1826

Floral Expression & Designs
Nevis Street
Tel: 463-8186

Flower World Ltd
Cnr St John's & Popeshead Streets
Tel: 562-9229

Grace Arbor
Upper Church Street
St John's
Tel: 461-0333

Lois E. Warner Designs Inc
P.O. Box W123
Tel: 562-6960 / 464-5335

Vison Holdings Ltd.
Market & Redcliffe Streets
Tel: 562-5256

FREIGHT FORWARDING

D&J Forwarders
51 Vegetable Market
Tel: 461-9766

Inter-Freight Ltd
V.C. Bird International Airport
Tel: 481-1200

Vernon G. Edwards
Cnr Thames & Long Streets
St John's
Tel: 462-2034

GOLF COURSES

Cedar Valley Golf Club Ltd.
Cedar Valley
Tel: 462-0161

Jolly Harbour Beach Resort Marina
& Golf Club
Jolly Harbour
Tel: 462-3085

GUESTHOUSES

A&G Guest House
Skerritts Pasture
Tel: 561-2804

Cappuccino Lounge
Nelson's Alley
Tel: 562-6808

Cedar Hill Cottages Ltd
Factory Road
Tel: 729-6411

Hillside Suites
Union Estate
Tel: 560-2187

Willowby Heights Guest House
St Phillips Village
Tel: 560-9738

HELICOPTER SERVICES

Caribbean Helicopters Ltd
Jolly Harbour
Tel: 460-5900

HOSPITALS

Holberton Hospital
Queen Elizabeth Highway
Tel: 462-0251 / 2 / 3 / 4
Fax: 462-4067

HOTELS

Antigua Hotel & Tourist Association
Lower Newgate Street
Tel: 462-0374
Fax: 462-3702
Email: ahta@candw.ag

Admirals Inn
Nelson's Dockyard
Tel: 460-1027
Fax: 460-1534
Email: admirals@candw.ag

Airport Hotel
Airport Road
Tel: 462-1191
Fax: 462-0928

Allegro Resort
Pineapple Beach
Tel: 463-2006
Fax: 463-2452
Email: info@antigua.allegroresorts

Amaryllis Hotel
Airport Road
Tel: 462-8690
Fax: 462-8691

Anchorage Inn
McKinnons
Tel: 462-4065
Fax: 462-4066
Email:
info@antiguaanchorageinn.com

Antigua Village Condo Beach Resort
Dickenson Bay
Tel: 462-2930. Fax: 462-0375
Email: antiguavillage@candw.ag

Antigua Yacht Club Marina & Resort
Falmouth Harbour
Tel: 460-1544
Fax: 460-1444
Email: aycmresort@candw.ag

Beachcomber Hotel
Winthropes Bay
Tel: 462-3100. Fax: 462-4012
Email: beachcom@candw.ag

The Beach House Barbuda
Palmetto Point, Barbuda
Tel: 725-4042
Fax: (212) 202 3939
Email:
info@thebeachhousebarbuda.com

Bikinis
Sandhaven
Tel: 562-5550
Fax: 462-4491

Blue Waters Hotel
Soldiers Bay
Tel: 462-0290
Fax: 462-0293
Email: bluewaters@candw.ag

Caribbean Inn & Suites
Radio Range
Tel: 562-0210

Carlisle Bay
Old Road Village
Tel: 484-0000
Fax: 562-5113
Email: info@carlisle-bay.com

Catamaran Hotel & Marina
Falmouth Harbour
Tel: 460-1036
Fax: 460-1506

Chez Pascal French Restaurant &
Deluxe Rooms
Galley Bay
Tel: 462-3232
Fax: 460-5730

City View Hotel & Restaurant
Newgate Street
St John's
Tel: 562-1211
Fax: 562-0242

Cocobay Resort
Valley Church
Tel: 562-2400
Fax: 562-2424
Email: cocobay@candw.ag

Coconut Beach Club
Yeptons Estate
Tel: 462-2520
Fax: 462-3240
Email:
coconutbeachclub@reservations.com

Coco Point Lodge
Codrington
Barbuda
Tel: 462-3816
Fax: 462-5340

Cocos
Valley Road
Tel: 462-9700. Fax: 462-9423
Email: cocos@candw.ag

Copper & Lumber Store Hotel
Nelson's Dockyard
Tel: 460-1058. Fax: 460-1529

Cortsland Hotel
Upper Gambles
Tel: 462-1395. Fax: 462-1699

Curtain Bluff Hotel
Old Road
Tel: 462-8400
Fax: 462-8409
Email: curtainbluff@candw.ag

Dickenson Bay Cottages
Tel: 462-4940. Fax: 462-4941

Dian Bay Resort & Spa
Dian Bay
Tel: 460-6646
Fax; 460-8400
Email: dianbay@candw.ag

Dove Cove
Dry Hill
Tel: 463-8600
Fax: 463-8601
Email: dovecove@candw.ag

Ellen Bay Cottages
Seatons
Tel: 561-2003
Website: www.ellenbaycottages.com

Emerald Spring Villas
Brown's Bay
Tel: 461-6323
Email:
info@emeraldspringsvillas.com

Galleon Beach Club
English Harbour
Tel: 460-1024
Fax: 460-1450
Email: galleonbeach@candw.ag

Galley Bay Resort
Five Islands
Tel: 462-0302
Fax: 462-4551
Email: reservations@antigua-resorts.com

Grand Royal Antiguan Beach Resort
Deep Bay
Tel: 462-3733
Fax: 462-3732
Email:
admin@grandroyalantiguan.com

Harbour View Apartments
Dockyard
Tel: 463-1026

Harmony Hall
Brown's Bay
Tel: 460-4120
Fax: 460-4406

HBK Villas
Jolly Harbour
Tel: 462-6166 / 67
Email: jollyhbr@candw.ag

Hawksbill by Rex Resorts
Five Islands
Tel: 462-0301
Fax: 462-1515
Email: hawksbill@candw.ag

Heritage Hotel
Heritage Quay
Tel: 462-1247
Fax: 462-1179
Email: heritagehotel@candw.ag

Hermitage Bay Hotel
P.O. Box 60
St John's, Antigua
Tel: 562-5500
Fax: 562-5505
Email: info@hermitagebay.com

The Inn at English Harbour
English Harbour
Tel: 460-1014
Fax: 460-1603
Email: theinn@candw.ag

Joe Mike's Downtown Hotel Plaza
Nevis Street
Tel: 462-1142
Fax: 462-6056
Email: joemikes@candw.ag

Jolly Beach Resort
Bolans Village
Tel: 462-0061
Fax: 562-2302
Email: info@jollybeachresort.com

Jolly Castle Hotel
Jolly Harbour
Tel: 463-9001
Fax: 462-9033

Jolly Harbour Villas
Jolly Harbour
Tel: 462-7771 / 2 / 3
Fax: 462-4900
Email:
hkupin@jollyharbourantigua.com

Jumby Bay Resort
Long Bay Island
Tel: 462-6000
Fax: 462-6020
Email: jumby@candw.ag

K Club
Barbuda
Tel: 460-0300
Fax: 460-0305
Email: kclubbarbuda@candw.ag

Long Bay Hotel
Long Bay
Tel: 463-2005
Fax: 463-2439
Email: longbay@candw.ag

Lord Nelson Beach Hotel
Dutchman's Bay
Tel: 462-3094
Fax: 462-3094

Mamora Resorts
Mamora Bay
Tel: 722 0306

Marina Bay Resort
Dickenson Bay
Tel: 462-3254 / 58. Fax: 462-2151
Email: marinabay@candw.ag

Mill Reef Club
PO Box 133
Mill Reef
Tel: 460 4290. Fax: 460 4298

Ocean Inn
English Harbour
Tel: 460-1263
Fax: 463-7950
Email: oceaninn@candw.ag

Palm Bay
Browns Bay
Tel: 460-4173
Email:
reservations@palmbayantigua.com

Pelican Isle
Johnson's Point
Tel: 462-8385
Fax: 462-4361
Email: pelican@candw.ag

Pigottsville Hotel
Wireless Road.
Tel: 462-0592

Rex Blue Heron
Johnsons Point
Tel: 462-8564
Fax: 462-8005

Rex Halcyon Cove
Dickenson Bay
Tel: 462-0256
Fax: 462-0271
Email: rexhalcyon@candw.ag

St James's Club
Mamora Bay
Tel: 460-0500
Fax: 460-3015
Email: reservations@antigua-resorts.com

Sandals Antigua Grand Resort & Spa
Dickenson Bay
Tel: 462-0267
Fax: 462-4135
Email: sandals@candw.ag

Sandpiper Reef Resort
Crosbies
Tel: 462-0939. Fax: 462-1743
Email: sandpiper@candw.ag

Serendipity Exclusive Vacation
Cottages
Freemans Village
Tel: 562-6500
Fax: 562-6502

Siboney Beach Club
Dickenson Bay
Tel: 462-0806. Fax: 462-3356
Email: siboney@candw.ag

South Coast Horizons
Cades Bay
Tel: 562-4074
Fax: 562-562-4075
Email:
admin@southcoasthorizons.com

The Suites at Jolly Beach Vacations
Bolans Village
Tel: 562-5185. Fax: 562-5184
Email:
info@jollybeachvacations.com

Sunsail Club Colonna
Hodges Bay
Tel: 462-6263. Fax: 462-6430
Email: colonna@candw.ag

Three Martini Beach Bar Restaurant
& Apartments
Crabbe Hill
Tel: 460-9306
Fax: 481-1735

Tradewinds Hotel
Dickenson Bay
Tel: 462-1223
Fax: 462-5007
Email: twhotel@candw.ag

Valley Creek Hotel & Fitness Centre
Valley Road
Tel: 722-0310

Willowby Heights Apartments
St Philip's Village
Tel: 460-4105
Fax: 560-9738

IMMIGRATION

Immigration Department
General Office, Queen Elizabeth
Highway
Tel: 562-1387
Fax: 562-1388

Crabbs: 463-3912
Deep Water Harbour: 462-9483
Dockyard: 463-9410
Heritage Quay: 462-7932
Jolly Harbour: 462-3590

INSURANCE COMPANIES

ABI Insurance Ltd
Redcliffe Street
Tel: 480-2825
Fax: 480-2834

American Life Insurance Co.
7 Woods Shopping Centre
Friars Hill Road
Tel: 462-2042
Fax: 462-2466

Anjo Insurances
Woods Centre
Tel: 480-3050
Fax: 480-3064

Antigua Insurance Company Ltd
Long Street
Tel: 480-9000
Fax: 480-9035

British American Insurance Co Ltd
Redcliffe Street
Tel: 481-5050
Fax: 481-5090

Brysons Insurance Agency
Long Street
Tel: 480-1220. Fax: 462-5538

Capital Insurance Ltd
Lwr. St John's Street
Tel: 562-0068
Fax: 562-0068

Caribbean Alliance
Long and Temple Streets
St John's
Tel: 481-2900
Fax: 481-2950
Email:
gregory.manners@caribbeanalliance.com

Clico International Life Insurance Ltd
Cnr Redcliffe Street
Tel: 480-3250
Fax: 480-3270

Kelsick Insurance Agency
The Vineyard
Redcliffe Street
Tel: 462-0049
Fax: 462-9441

Khouly Alliance Group
P.O. Box 511
Tel: 480-9000
Fax: 480-9035
Email: anicol@candw.ag

NEM (West Indies) Insurance Ltd
High Street
Tel: 481-1850
Fax: 481-1859

United Insurance Co. Ltd
Woods Centre
Tel: 480-3050
Fax: 480-3064

INTERNET CAFES

Antigua Cyberstop
Antigua Yacht Club Marina
Falmouth Harbour
Tel: 463-2662
Fax: 562-2225

BBR Sports Bar
Tel: 462-6260
Fax: 460-8182
Email: rpool10405@aol.com

Cyber Centre
Newgate Street
Tel: 462-2638
Fax: 462-2658

First Internet Café
Upper Redcliffe Street
Tel: 562-5312
Fax: 562-5313

Internet Connections
Upper High Street
Tel: 480-3000
Fax: 480-3003

Jolly Home Hardware & Services
Jolly Harbour
Tel: 562-2377
Fax: 562-2409

Kangaroo Express
Redcliffe Street
St John's
Tel: 562-3895
Fax: 562-3895

Mad Max
Dickenson Bay
Tel: 562-4653
Fax: 562-4653

Skullduggery Café
Tel: 463-0625
Email:
skullduggerycafe@hotmail.com

JEWELLERS

Abbotts Jewellery
Heritage Quay
Tel: 462-3107 / 8
Fax: 462-3109
Email: abbots@candw.ag

Antigua Jewellers
Market & Redcliffe Streets
Tel: 462-2988. Fax: 462-2988

Baileys Jewellers
North Street
Tel: 462-2070

Colombian Emeralds International
Heritage Quay
Tel: 462-7903
Fax: 462-3351
Email: cmatthews@dutyfree.com

Diamonds International
Heritage Quay
Tel: 481-1880. Fax: 481-1899

The Goldsmitty
Redcliffe Quay
Tel: 462-4601. Fax; 462-3789

Jewellers Warehouse
Heritage Quay
Tel: 462-2336
Fax: 463-2343

Luxury Brands
Heritage Quay
Tel: 562-5612. Fax: 562-5611

Lyan's Jewellery
Cnr Market & Redcliffe Streets
Tel: 562-1596
Fax: 462-2988

Passions Jewellery
Heritage Quay
Tel: 562-5295
Fax: 562-5298

Sterlings
Heritage Quay
Tel: 562-5662
Fax: 562-5664

Timeless Treasures
Heritage Quay
Tel: 462-5588
Fax: 462-5587

LAUNDRIES & DRY CLEANERS

Burton's Laundromat & Dry
Cleaning
Independence Drive & Jolly Harbour
Tel: 462-4268
Fax: 462-3177

Maude's Laundry
All Saints Village
Tel: 460-2902

O'Beez Laundromat & Cleaners
Factory Road
Tel: 462-4661

Reynolds Laundry
All Saints & Warren Road
Tel: 462-2519

Sam & Dave Laundry
English Harbour
Tel: 460-1266

Snow White Laundry
Parham Town
Tel: 463-2061

LIBRARIES

Antigua & Barbuda Public Library
Market Street
Tel: 462-0229

Law Library
St Mary's & Temple Streets
Tel: 462-0626

LIQUOR, BEER & WINE RETAILERS

Antigua Distillery Ltd
Friars Hill Road
St John's
Tel: 480-3200
Fax: 480-3215
Email: info@antiguadistillery.com

Best Cellars Wines & spirits
Airport Road
Tel: 480-5180. Fax: 480-5185

Crab Hole Liquors
Cobbs Cross
St Paul's
Tel: 460-1212
Fax: 460-8930
Email: crabholeliquors@candw.ag

Dockside Liquors & Supermarket
Antigua Yacht Club Marina
English Harbour
Tel: 463-9000

Kennedy's Liquor World Ltd
Lwr Market Street
Tel: 481-1300
Fax: 481-1325

The Liquor Shop
Heritage Quay
Tel: 462-2606
Fax: 462-4244

Premier Beverages
Friar's Hill Road
Tel: 480-3200
Fax: 480-3215

Quin Farara & Co Ltd
P.O. Box 215
St John's
Tel: 462-3198
Fax: 462-3876
Email: quinfarara@candw.ag

MAIL FORWARDING SERVICES

Mail Boxes Etc
Old Parham Road
Tel: 562-5090
Fax: 562-5089

WinBox
High & Temple Streets
Tel: 460-3661
Fax: 460-3662

Xpress Courier
M & M Ave
Old Parham Road
Tel: 462-1197
Fax: 560-9647

MARINAS

Antigua Slipway
English Harbour
Tel: 460-1056

Antigua Yacht Club Marina Resort &
Restaurant
Falmouth Harbour
Tel: 460-1544
Fax: 460-1444

Catamaran Marina
Falmouth Harbour
Tel: 460-1503

Falmouth Harbour Marina
Falmouth Harbour
Tel: 460-6054. Fax: 460-6055

Jolly Harbour Beach Resort Marina
& Golf Club
Jolly Harbour
Tel: 462-3085
Fax: 462-7703

Nelson's Dockyard Marina
Nelsons Dockyard
Tel: 460-7976

St John's Dock
Redcliffe Quay
Tel: 562-1960

Shell Beach Marina
Shell Beach
Tel: 562-0185
Fax: 463-5255

MARINE EQUIPMENT & SUPPLIES

Antigua Slipway
English Harbour
Tel: 460-1056

Antigua Yacht Service
Dockyard Drive
Tel: 460-1121

Budget Marine
Jolly Harbour
Tel: 462-8753
Fax: 460-8625

Catamaran Marina
Falmouth Harbour
Tel: 460-1503

Falmouth Harbour Marine Services
English Harbour
Tel: 463-8081

Island Motors Ltd
St John's
Tel: 462-2163

Paradise Boat Sales & Marine
Centre
Old Parham Road
Tel: 562-7125. Fax: 562-9651

Sands Trading
Jolly Harbour
Tel: 462-7962

The Signal Locker
English Harbour
Tel: 460-1528

MARINE REPAIR SERVICES

A-1 Marine Services
Jolly Harbour
Tel: 462-7755

Antigua Marine Services Ltd.
Shell Beach
Tel: 562-3499. Fax: 562-3499

MEDICAL CENTRES

Adelin Medical Centre Ltd
Fort Road
Tel: 462-0866. Fax: 462-2386

MONEY TRANSFERS

Cyber Vision Money Transfer
Gray Hill
Tel: 562-5848

Laparkan Antigua Ltd
Bencorp Building
Independence Dr
Tel: 562-5314
Fax: 562-5316

Moneygram International Money
Transfer
Long & Thames Street
Tel: 481-2700
Fax: 481-2710

Transfer Plus
Weathered Complex
Redcliffe Street
Tel: 562-5875

MORTGAGE COMPANIES

ACB Mortgage & Trust Co. Ltd
High & Temple Streets
Tel: 481-4300. Fax: 481-4313

Caribbean Finance & Mortgage Co
Woods Centre
Friars Hill Road
Tel: 462-9215. Fax: 462-9214

National Mortgage & Trust Co Ltd
Upper High Street
Tel: 462-9497
Fax: 462-9496

MOTORCYCLE & MOTOR SCOOTER RENTALS

JT's Rent-A-Scoot
Tel: 774-1905

Paradise Boat Sales
Tel: 460-7125

Sun Cycles Bicycle Rental
Hodges Bay
Tel: 461-0324

Shipwreck Rent-A-Scooter
Dockyard Drive
Tel: 460-6087

Tropical Rentals
Tel: 562-5180

NATIONAL PARKS

Dows Hill Historic Centre
Dows Hill
Tel: 481-5045

National Parks Authority
Nelsons Dockyard
Tel: 481-5022
Email: natpark@candw.ag

NEWSAGENTS
(see Booksellers & Newsagents)

NEWSPAPERS & MAGAZINES

Antigua Sun
Coolidge
Tel: 480-5960
Fax: 480-5968
Email: editor@antiguasun.com

Daily Observer
Coolidge
Tel: 480-1750
Fax: 480-1757
Email: dailyobserver@candw.ag

Sun Weekend
Coolidge
Tel: 480-5960
Fax: 480-5968
Email: editor@antiguasun.com

NIGHTCLUBS

Abracadabra Bar & Restaurant
English Harbour
Tel: 460-2701

The Beach
Dickenson Bay
Tel: 480-6940

Big Banana
Redcliffe Quay
St John's
Tel: 480-6985

By Betty Rustic Eatery & By Betty
Outdoors
Factory Road
Tel: 764-0151
Fax: 461-8726

C&C Wine Bar
Redcliffe Quay
Tel: 460-7025
Fax: 561-0221

Catcus Bar & Restaurant
Falmouth
Tel: 460-6575

Club Havana Mexican Catina & Bar
English Harbour
725-2308

Club Savoy
Old Parham Road
562-6219

The Coast
Heritage Quay
Tel: 562-6278

Coconut Grove Restaurant & Beach
Bar
Dickenson Bay
Tel: 462-1538

Dogwatch Tavern
Jolly Harbour
Tel: 462-6550

Grand Princess
Jolly Harbour
Tel: 562-9900

Joe Mike's Hotel
Cnr Nevis Street & Corn Alley
Tel: 462-1142

King's Casino
Heritage Quay
Tel: 462-1727

Last Lemming Bar & Restaurant
Falmouth Harbour
Tel: 460-6910

Liquid Nightclub
2nd Floor Grand Princess
Jolly Harbour
Tel: 562-7874

Mad Mongoose
Falmouth Harbour
Tel: 463-7900

The New 18 Karat Night Club Bar &
Restaurant
Lwr Church Street
Tel: 562-1858
Fax: 460-7587

O'Grady's Pub
Redcliffe Street
Tel: 462-5392

Rush Nightclub
Runaway Bay
Tel: 562-7874

Spliff Bar & Grill
Old Parham Road
Tel: 562-5138

Steely Bar BBR Sportive
Jolly Harbour
Tel: 462-6260

OFFSHORE SERVICES

Antigua Corporate Management
Services
Woods
Tel: 460-6872

Antigua International Trust Ltd
Woods Centre
Tel: 480-2313

Antigua Offshore Inc
44 Church Street
Tel: 462-5233
Fax: 462-5234

OPTICIANS, OPHTHALMOLOGISTS & OPTOMETRISTS

Dr Jillia Bird
Milburn House
Old Parham Road
Tel: 462-1513
Fax: 462-5622

Dr Alvin Edwards
Upper Redcliffe Street
St John's
Tel: 462-2748
Fax: 462-1976

Progressive Vision
Old Parham Road
Tel: 562-6265
Fax: 481-1707

Karen Roberts
Eyeland Optical
Woods Mall
Friars Hill Road
Tel: 462-2020
Fax: 460-5095

Vision Express
Upper Redcliffe Street
Tel: 462-2748
Fax: 462-1976

Dr Ian Walwyn
Stapleton Lane Clinic
Tel: 562-1931

Dr R A Walwyn
Stapleton Lane Medical Clinic
Tel: 462-0031
Fax: 462-0031

PHARMACIES

Alpha Pharmacy
Redcliffe Street
Tel: 462-1112

Ceco Pharmacy
High Street
Tel: 562-4706
Fax: 562-3273

City Pharmacy
St Mary's Street
Tel: 480-3314 . Fax: 480-3313

Cornerstone Pharmacy
Upper Newgate Street
Tel: 462-7859

Dyett Pharmacy
Cross Street
Tel: 462-0925

EVC Health & Beauty Store
Lower New Street
Tel: 562-4545

Food City Pharmacy
Deep Water Harbour
Tel: 462-4808
Fax: 480-8729

Grace Green Pharmacy
Christian Street
Tel: 463-0888

Health Pharmacy
Redcliffe Street
Tel: 462-1255

Hill's Drug Mart
Long Street
Tel: 460-6710

JFK Pharmacy
Long Street
Tel: 562-1621

Liberty Pharmacy
Liberta Village
Tel: 460-4994

Medical Benefits Scheme
Nevis Street
Tel: 462-1621
Fax: 462-3318

Natures Family Store (Family
Pharmacy)
Lower Market Street
Tel: 462-1153
Fax: 460-6890

Old Nox Pharmacy
Jardines Court
St Mary's Street
Tel: 562-4721. Fax: 562-4721

People's Pharmacy
Corn Alley
Tel: 462-2214. Fax: 462-2214

Piper's Pharmacy
All Saints Road
Tel: 462-0736
Fax: 462-0736

Ramco Pharmacy
Camacho's Avenue
Tel: 462-2944

Reliance Pharmacy
Redcliffe Street
Tel: 462-4646
Fax: 462-4874

Shopper's Pharmacy Ltd
High Street
St John's
Tel: 462-4706. Fax: 462-7779

Stevens Pharmacy
Temple & Redcliffe Streets
Tel: 462-2214

Super Drug Store
Popeshead & Bishopgate Streets
Tel: 460-5018

Sysco Pharmacy
Jolly Harbour
Tel: 462-5917
Fax: 562-8204

Triton Pharmacy
Ramco Building
Camacho's Avenue
Tel: 462-2944

Woods Pharmacy
Woods Centre
Tel: 462-9287
Fax: 462-9289

PHOTOGRAPHERS & PHOTOGRAPHY STUDIOS

Alexis Andrew
English Harbour
Tel: 460-1175

Benjies
Redcliffe Street
Tel: 462-0733

Carib Photo
Woods Centre
Tel: 562-0142

Hot Shot Photo
Sandals Resort
Tel: 463-8648
Fax: 460-9646

Image Locker
Nelsons Dockyard
Tel: 460-1246

Images.Cam Photo Studio
Redcliffe Quay
Tel: 463-6099

Island Photo
Redcliffe Street
St John's
Tel: 462-1567
Fax: 462-7726

Jackal Photo Studio
Wireless Road
Tel: 462-0640

Joseph Jones Photography
Ffryes Estate
Tel: 462-7317
Cell: 774-7317

Ken Maguire
Liberta
Tel: 460-1835

Photogenesis Imaging
Michael's Avenue
Tel: 462-1066
Fax: 562-2901

Photo Shak Ltd
St John's
Tel: 773-9084. Fax: 562-1052

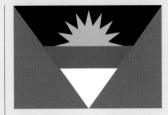

Skip's Photo Studio
St Mary's Street
St John's
Tel: 462-5878
Fax: 462-5878

Soul Train Photo Studio
Vivian Richards Street
St John's
Tel: 462-0850

Tots Plus Photo Studio
Tel: 462-9588
Fax: 462-9588

Tropical Studios
Falmouth
Tel: 460-1235

PHOTOGRAPHIC EQUIPMENT & SERVICES

Images.cam Photo Studio
23 Redcliffe Quay
St John's
Tel: 463-6009

Island Photo
Redcliffe Street
St John's
Tel: 462-1567
Fax: 462-7726

Photogenesis Imaging
Michael's Avenue
Tel: 462-1066
Fax: 562-2901

PHYSIOTHERAPISTS

Christine Gillis-Gerrad
Physiotherapist
c/o Equilibrium
Marble Hill
Tel: 560-3780

Denis J Gobinet
Physiotherapist
Crosbies
Tel: 462-2231

Dr Patrick Matthew
NSA Medical Centre
Tel: 462-0631
Fax: 462-0631

PORT AUTHORITIES

Antigua Port Authority
Deep Water Harbour
Tel: 462-3439

Immigration Office
Deep Water Harbour: 462-0050
Jolly Harbour: 462-7931

POLICE

Royal Police Force of Antigua &
Barbuda (Headquarters)
American Road
Tel: 462-0125 / 6 / 7
Fax: 462-0954

POST OFFICE

General Post Office
High & Long Streets
Tel: 562-1928
Fax: 460-9650

RADIO STATIONS

ABS Radio
Old Parham Road
Tel: 462-2998
Fax: 562-2801
Email: absradio@ab.gov.ag

CANA News
Tel: 460-2458
Fax: 460-2458
Email: colo_tintin@hotmail.com

Crusader Radio
Redcliffe Street
St John's
Tel: 562-4911
Fax: 562-4613
Email: crusadernews@candw.ag

Family Radio
Tel: 560-7578
Fax: 560-7577
Email: family@caribmail.com

Gem Radio
Tel: 462-6222
Fax: 462-6224
Email: gemradio@candw.ag

Hitz FM
Ryan's Building
High Street
Tel: 562-4489

Observer Radio 911
High Street
Tel: 481-9100
Fax: 481-9125
Email: voice@radio911fm.com

Red Hot Radio
Carlisle
Tel: 562-9850

Sun FM / ZDK Radio
Ottos
Tel: 462-1101
Fax: 462-1111
Email: zdknews@hotmail.com

REAL ESTATE AGENTS

ABI Realty
St John's
Tel: 460-9707
Fax: 460-9707

Antigua Estates
Jolly Harbour
Tel: 562-5622. Fax: 562-5623

Antigua Luxury Homes Ltd
St John's
Tel: 562-6565. Fax: 560-7722

Antigua Tropical Heritage Realty
English Harbour
Tel: 560-6332. Fax: 560-6332

Caribbean Real Estate Agency Ltd
Dian Point
Tel: 562-5644

Haynes Smith Real Estate Agency
St John's
Tel: 462-5605
Fax: 462-5605

JABS Real Estate & Auctioneers
St John's
Tel: 562-6561. Fax: 562-6561

JCM Real Estate Investment
Bolans Village
Tel: 560-9013

Knight Brothers Real Estate
St John's
Tel: 462-0100
Fax: 461-1165

SE Realty Ltd
St John's
Tel: 562-3130
Fax: 562-3130

RESTAURANTS

Abracadraba Restaurant
English Harbour
Tel: 460-1732

Afiamani Creole Cuisine Restaurant
Temple Street
Tel: 562-5855

Admirals Inn
Nelsons Dockyard
Tel: 460-1027

Alberto's Restaurant
Willoughby Bay
Tel: 460-3007
Fax: 460-3007

Al Porto Restaurant
Jolly Harbour
Tel: 462-7695

Amigo's Mexican Restaurant
Runaway Bay
Tel: 562-1545
Fax: 461-3304

Antigua Yacht Club Marina
Restaurant
Falmouth Harbour
Tel: 460-1797
Fax: 460-1444

Barry's Café & Bakery
Long Street
Tel: 562-4310
Fax: 562-4310

Bayhouse Restaurant
Tradewinds Hotel
Tel: 462-1223
Fax: 462-5007

The Beach
Dickenson Bay
Tel: 480-6940. Fax: 480-6943

Bellyful
Lower All Saints Road
Tel: 562-4098. Fax: 562-4099

Best Health Vegetarian Restaurant
Airport Road
Tel: 462-1933

Big Banana 1761 (Airport
Restaurant)
V C Bird International Airport
Tel: 480-6979. Fax: 480-6999

Big Banana Holding Co Ltd (Pizzas)
Redcliffe Quay
Tel: 480-6985. Fax 480-6989

Billigins Bar & Restaurant
Camacho Ave
Tel: 462-3556

Blue Waters Hotel
Blue Waters
Tel: 462-0290
Fax: 462-0293

Boardwalk Bar & Grill
Heritage Quay
St John's
Tel: 562-3231
Fax: 562-3233

Bocciolo Italian Restaurant
Jolly Beach Resort
Tel: 462-0061
Fax: 562-2302

Bounce Castle Restaurant
Paynters
Tel: 562-4541

Café Napolean
Redcliffe Quay
Tel: 562-1820

Calypso Restaurant
Airport Road
Tel: 562-3067

Cap Horn Restaurant & Pizza
English Harbour
Tel: 460-1194

Cappuccino Lounge
Nelson's Alley
Tel: 562-6808
Fax: 562-6802

Caribbean Taste Restaurant
English Harbour
Tel: 562-3049

Catherine's Café
English Harbour
Tel: 460-5050

Catherine's Corner Jamaican
Restaurant
Newgate Street
Tel: 562-5955

Charissma
St John's Street
St John's
Tel: 562-2228

Chez Pascal French Restaurant
Galley Bay
Tel: 462-3232
Fax: 460-5730

Chicken Hut
Cnr Long Street & Soul Alley
Tel: 562-4107
Fax: 562-1258

City View Hotel & Restaurant
Newgate Street
St John's
Tel: 562-1211
Fax: 562-0242

Claudia's Place
Long Street
Tel: 562-1060

Coconut Grove Restaurant & Beach
Bar
Dickenson Bay
Tel: 462-1538. Fax: 462-2162

Cocos Hotel & Restaurant
Valley Road
Tel: 462-9700
Fax: 462-9423

Colombo's Italian Restaurant
Galleon Beach
Tel: 460-1452. Fax: 460-1450

Commissioner Grill
Redcliffe Street
Tel: 462-1883
Fax: 462-1856

The Cove
Boons Point
Soldier Bay
Tel: 562-2683

Creole Beach Bar Restaurant
Crabbe Hill
Tel: 562-2218

Delightful Chinese Restaurant
Upper St Mary's Street
Tel: 462-5780
Fax: 562-4286

The Docksider
St James's Club
Tel: 460-5000

Downtown Food Mall
Cnr High & Market Streets
Tel: 460-8474

Elpert's Café
Lower Long Street
Tel: 460-2233
Fax: 560-2233

El Taco Loco
Nevis Street
Tel: 562-8226
Fax: 562-8227

Famous Mauros Bar & Restaurant
Pizzeria
English Harbour
Tel: 460-1318

Fandango Bar & Restaurant
Market Street
Tel: 462-4272

Fojee's Restaurant
All Saints Road
Tel: 462-2406

Galley Restaurant
Nelson's Dockyard
Tel: 460-1533

George Restaurant
Market Street
Tel: 562-4866
Fax: 562-4866

The Golden Bowl Restaurant
Church Street
Tel: 462-4505

Grace Before Meals
English Harbour
Tel: 460-1298

The Green Door Tavern
Madison's Square, Barbuda
Tel: 562-3134

Green Garden Restaurant & Bar
High Street
Tel: 562-2500

Harbour Café
Jolly Harbour
Tel: 462-6026

Harmony Hall
Brown's Bay
Tel: 460-4120
Fax: 460-4406

Hemisphere International
Restaurant
Jolly Beach
Tel: 462-0061
Fax: 562-2302

Hemmingway's Caribbean Café
St Mary's Street
St John's
Tel: 462-2763

Home Restaurant
Gambles
Tel: 461-7651. Fax: 461-0277

Honeycutter
Upper Nevis Street
Tel: 562-6671

HQ Restaurant & Bar
Nelson's Dockyard
Tel: 562-2563

Jazzie'z
Valley Church Beach
Tel: 560-2582. Fax: 560-5182

Jimmy's
Catamaran, Falmouth
Tel: 463-8866

Joe Mike's Hotel Plaza
Nevis Street
Tel: 462-1142
Fax: 462-6056
E: mail: joemikes@candw.ag

Julian's Alfresco
Barrymore Beach Club
Runaway Bay
Tel: 562-1545. Tel: 460-1662

Kalabashe #10
Vendors Mall
Tel: 562-6070

Kentucky Fried Chicken (KFC) Ltd
High Street & Fort Road
Tel: 462-1951 / 9415
Fax: 462-3485

La Perruche Restaurant
English Harbour
Tel: 460-3040

Last Lemmins Bar & Restaurant
Falmouth Harbour
Tel: 460-6910

Le Bistro French Restaurant
Hodges Bay
Tel: 462-3881
Fax: 461-2996
Email: pgbistro@candw.ag

Le Cap Horn
English Harbour
Tel: 460-1194
Fax: 460-1793

Lobster Shack
Runaway Bay
Tel: 462-2855
Fax: 462-7966

Lord Nelson Beach Hotel
Dutchman's Bay, Coolidge
Tel: 462-3094
Fax: 462-3094

Lydia's Caribbean Seafood
Restaurant
Jolly Beach Hotel
Tel: 462-0061
Fax: 562-2302

Mama Lolly's Vegetarian Café
Redcliffe Quay
Tel: 562-1552
Fax: 562-1552

Melini's Ristorante / Pizzeria
Jolly Harbour
Tel: 562-4173. Fax: 560-8952

Mid East Fast Food
Upper Newgate Street & Redcliffe
Quay
Tel: 562-0101. Fax: 560-9595

Miller's by the Sea
Fort James
Tel: 462-9414. Fax: 462-9591

Natural N'yam Vegetarian
Restaurant
Cross Street
Tel: 562-0174

New Thriving Chinese Restaurant
Long Street / Airport Road
Tel: 462-4611 / 562-0046

O'Grady's Pub
Redcliffe Street
St John's
Tel: 462-5392

O J's Bar & Restaurant
Crabbe Hill
Tel: 460-0184

The Palm Restaurant
Blue Waters Hotel
Tel: 462-0290

Palm Tree Restaurant
Barbuda
Tel: 460-0517

Papa Zouk Fish & Rum
Upper Gambles
Tel: 464-7576 / 6044

Papi's
Fort Road
Tel: 562-7274

Pari's Pizza & Steakhouse
Tradewinds
Tel: 462-1501. Fax: 461-1508

The Pavilion
Coolidge
Tel: 481-6800

Peter's BBQ & Steakhouse
Jolly Harbour
Tel: 462-6026

Philtons Bakery Café
Friars Hill Road
Tel: 463-2253

Pita Pocket & Snack
Nevis Street
Tel: 562-4136
Fax: 463-6885

The Pitch Bar & Restaurant
Coolidge
Tel: 461-1417 / 462-1417

Pizza Oven
Dockyard Drive
Tel: 562-6020

Rainbow's End Restaurant
Bolans Village
Tel: 562-2789

Red Octopus Seafood Restaurant
English Harbour
Tel: 460-1882

Roti King
St Mary's Street
Tel: 462-2328

Russell's Fort James Seafood
Restaurant
Fort James
Tel: 462-5479

Saffron Restaurant
Grand Princess
Tel: 562-4781

Sea Breeze Café
Antigua Yacht Club
Tel: 562-3739

Sheer at Cocobay Resort
Cocobay Resort
Tel: 562-2400
Fax: 562-2424

The Shell Beach Pub
Coolidge
Tel: 461-1417
Tel: 462-1417

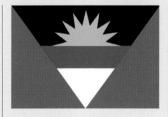

Shirley Heights Lookout
Shirley Heights
Tel: 460-1785

Skulduggery Café
Antigua Yacht Club Marina
Tel: 460-1444

Southern Cross Restaurant
Yacht Club
Tel: 460-1797. Fax: 460-1797

Southern Fry Restaurant
Lower Market Street & Old Parham
Road
Tel: 462-1616

Spliff Bar & Grill
Old Parham Road
Tel: 463-8611
Fax: 562-4553

Steely Bar & Restaurant at BBR
Sportive
Jolly Harbour
Tel: 462-6260. Fax: 460-8182

Sticky Wicket Restaurant & Bar
Coolidge
Tel: 481-7000
Fax: 481-7010

Subway
Redcliffe Street
Tel: 562-5539. Fax: 562-5539

The Terrace Restaurant
The Inn at English Harbour
Tel: 460-1014

Three Martini Beach Bar Restaurant
& Apartments
Crabbe Hill
Tel: 480-9306. Fax: 481-1735

Trappas Bar
Dockyard Drive
Tel: 562-3534

Turner's Beach Bar & Restaurant
Johnson's Point
Tel: 462-9133. Fax: 560-8114

Ustav
Jolly Beach Hotel
Tel: 462-0061. Fax: 562-2302

The Verandah Bar
Jumby Bay Resort
Tel: 462-6000

Vyvien's
Blue Waters Hotel
Tel: 462-0290

Warri Pier Restaurant
Rex Halcyon Cove
Tel: 462-0256. Fax: 462-0271

RIDING STABLES

Spring Hill Riding Club
Falmouth Harbour
Tel: 460-7787 / 460-1333
Fax: 460-1333
Email: eastonj@candw.ag

SHIPPING COMPANIES

Bryson's Shipping Agency
St John's
Tel: 480-1240
Fax: 462-0170

Caribseas Ltd
St John's
Tel: 462-4863
Fax: 462-4864
Email: caribsea@candw.ag

Consolidated Maritime Services Ltd
St John's
Tel: 462-1224
Fax: 462-1227
Email: caribms@candw.ag

Francis Trading Agency Ltd
St John's
Tel: 462-4555
Fax: 462-0849
Email: fta@candw.ag

Inter-Freight Ltd
St John's
Tel: 481-1200
Fax: 481-1216
Email: ifreight@candw.ag

Laparkan Antigua Ltd
St John's
Tel: 562-5314
Fax: 562-5316

Tropical Shipping
St John's
Tel: 562-2934
Fax: 562-2935

Vernon G Edwards
Cnr Thames & Long Streets
Tel: 462-2034
Fax: 462-2035

SHOPPING CENTRES

Woods Centre
Friars Hill Road, St John's
Tel: 462-9367

SIGHTSEEING TOUR OPERATORS

Bo Tours
Tel: 462-6632

Coral Island Tours
Redcliffe Quay
Tel: 460-5625

Estate Safari & Classic Jeep Tours
Tel: 463-2061. Fax: 463-4713

Global Travel & Tours
Long Street
Tel: 480-1001

International Travel Consultants Ltd
Thames & Church Streets
Tel: 462-0811
Fax: 462-4156

Mountain to Sea Bike Adventure
Paynters Estates
Tel: 770-4837

National Tours & Services
Tel: 462-7979

Novella's Travel & Tours
Yacht Club Marina Building
Tel: 460-1209

Tropical Adventures
Redcliffe Street
Tel: 480-1225
Fax: 462-2065

Tropical Trails
Fitches Creek
Tel: 461-0383

Tropikelly Trails
Tel: 461-0383

X O Tours
English Harbour
Tel: 460-8687

SPORTING GOODS

Heritage Sports
46 Heritage Quay
Tel: 462-2809
Fax: 462-4658

Rising Star
Market & St Mary's Street
Tel: 460-8490
Fax: 460-8491

TAXI SERVICES

Antigua Reliable 24hr Taxi Service
West Bus Station
Tel: 460-5353

Archibald Taxi Service
Powells
Tel: 562-1709

Brother's Taxi Service
Lower Long Street
Tel: 462-6464

Christo Taxi Stand
High Street
Tel: 460-7434

Co-operative Taxi Service
Villa
Tel: 462-4325

Daylight Taxi Service
Long Street
Tel: 462-3015

Gravy Taxi Stand
Market Street
Tel: 462-0711

Heritage Quay Taxi Stand
Heritage Quay
Tel: 460-8213

Life Saver Taxi Stand
Lower Tanner Street
Tel: 460-9898

Matthew Car Rental & Taxi Service
Tel: 462-8803

Reliable Taxi Service
Fax: 463-3955

Sandals Antigua Taxi Stand
Dickenson Bay
Tel: 462-2504

United Taxi Association
V C Bird International Airport
Tel: 562-0262

West Bus Station Taxi Service
Tel: 462-5190

TELECOMMUNICATIONS COMPANIES

Antigua Public Utilities Authority
Cassada Gardens
Tel: 480-7000
Email: apuaops@candw.ag

Cable & Wireless (WI) Ltd
Clare Hall
Tel: 480-4000
Fax: 480-4105

Digicel
Redcliffe Street & Woods Mall
Tel: 480-2075 / 480-2050

The Signal Locker
Nelson's Dockyard
Tel: 460-1528
Fax: 460-1148

TELEVISION STATIONS

ABS TV
Cross Street
Tel: 462-1233. Fax: 462-4442
Email: antiguatv@hotmail.com

CTV
Long Street
Tel: 462-4224
Fax: 462-4211

GIS News
Cross Street
Tel: 462-2869
Fax: 462-4442
Email: gisnews@hotmail.com

TOURISM MINISTRY

Ministry of Tourism & Aviation
Government Complex
Queen Elizabeth Highway
P.O. Box 363
Tel: 462-0480
Fax: 462-2483
Email: deptourism@antigua.gov.ag

National Parks Authority
Nelson's Dockyard
Tel: 481-5022
Fax: 481-5047
Email: natpark@candw.ag

TOURIST ATTRACTIONS

Cades Bay Pineapple Station
Old Road

Canopy Tours
Fig Tree Drive
Tel: 562-6363

Cenotaph
High Street, St John's

Betty's Hope Estate
Pares Village
Tel: 462-4930 / 1469

Fort Barrington
Deep Bay

Fort Berkley
English Harbour
Tel: 460-1379

Fort George
Monk's Hill
Tel: 460-1379

Government House / Governor
General's Residence
Independence Drive
Tel: 462-0003

Indian Town & Devil's Bridge
East Coast

Industrial School for the Blind
All Saints Road
Tel: 462-0663

National Archives
Factory Road
Tel: 462-3946 / 7

Nelson's Dockyard National Park
English Harbour
Tel: 481-5022

St John's Cathedral
Newgate & Long Streets

Stingray City Antigua Ltd
Seatons
Tel: 562-7297. Fax: 562-7297

Westerby Memorial
High Street, St John's

TOUR OPERATORS

Alexander Parrish (Antigua) Ltd
Thames Street
Tel: 462-0187. Fax: 462-4457

Antigua Vacations Ltd
Jardines Court
Tel: 460-7383. Fax: 4463-8959

Bo Tours
Tel: 462-6632
Fax: 462-5336

Coral Island Tours
Redcliffe Quay
Tel: 460-5625
Fax: 460-5626

Destination Antigua
Tel: 463-1944. Fax: 463-3344

Global Travel & Tours
High Street
Tel: 480-1230. Fax: 462-0320

International Travel Consultants
(ITC) Ltd
Thames & Church Street
Tel: 462-0811. Fax: 462-4156

National Tours
Tel: 462-7979. Fax: 462-7979

Nicholson's Travel Agency
English Harbour
Tel: 463-7391 / 2
Fax: 462-4802

Paradise Island Tours
Tel: 462-7208. Tel: 727-5632

SunTours
Cnr Long & Thames Street
Tel: 462-4788. Fax: 462-4799

Wadadli Travel & ToursLtd.
Tel: 462-2227 / 28. Fax: 462-4489

VILLA RENTALS & SALES

Brown's Bay Villas
Brown's Bay
Tel: 460-4174. Fax: 460-4175

CaribRep Villas
Tel: 463-2070. Fax: 560-1824

Cedar Hill Cottages
Cedar Hill
Tel: 729-6411

Island Rentals
English Harbour
Tel: 463-2662
Fax: 562-2225

WATER – BOTTLED & BULK

Antigua Home & Office Depot
Old Parham Road
Tel: 462-2403
Fax: 480-2390

Island Coolers
All Saints Road
Tel: 560-8718

Premier Beverages
Friars Hill Road.
Tel: 480-3200
Fax: 480-3215

WATER SPORTS

Adventure Antigua
Tel: 726-6355

Antigua Seafaris
Tel: 464-3571

Barbuda Express Ferry Service &
Day Tours
Tel: 560-7989

Black Swan Pirate Party Cruise
Redcliffe Quay
Tel: 562-7946

Deep Bay Divers
Redcliffe Quay
Tel: 463-8000. Fax: 463-8000

Dockyard Divers
Nelson's Dockyard
Tel: 460-1178. Fax: 460-5850

Dolphin Fantaseas
Tel: 562-7946

H2O Antigua Beach Club
Dutchman's Bay
Tel: 562-3933

Indigo Divers
Jolly Harbour
Tel: 729-3483

Island Speedboats Ltd
Jolly Harbour
Tel: 774-1810

Jolly Dive
Jolly Harbour
Tel: 462-8305

Jolly Harbour Watersports
Tel: 462-7979 / 774-3005

Kite Antigua
Jabberwok Beach
Tel: 727-3983

Long Bay Hotel
Long Bay
Tel: 463-2005

Missa Ferdie
Tel: 462-1440 / 460-1503

Nightwing
Tel: 464-4665

Obsession Deep Sea Fishing
Charters
Hodges Bay
Tel: 462-2824. Fax: 462-3496

Overdraft
Tel: 462-1961 / 464-4954

Paddles Kayak Eco Trips
Seaton's Village
Tel: 463-1944. Fax: 463-3344

Sandals
Dickenson Bay
Tel: 462-0267

Sea Spa Private Charters
Jolly Harbour
Tel: 726-1009

SeaSports – Sneakie Pete's
Dickenson Bay
Tel: 462-3355. Fax: 463-0722

Shore Tours Antigua
Dickenson Bay
Tel: 462-6326

Stingray City Antigua Ltd
Seaton's Village
Tel: 562-7297. Fax: 562-7297

Sunsail Club Colonna
Hodges Bay
Tel: 462-6263

Swalings International School of
Swimming
Jolly Harbour
Tel: 561-0707

Treasure Island Cruises
Five Islands
Tel: 461-8675

Wadadli Watersports
Lwr Fort Road
Tel: 462-4792

WEDDING SERVICES & SUPPLIES

Admirals Inn
Nelson's Dockyard
Tel: 460-1027. Fax: 460-1534
Email: admirals@candw.ag

Allegro Resort
Pineapple Beach
Tel: 463-2006. Fax: 463-2452
Email: info@antigua.allegroresorts

Annlins Bridal & Tuxedo
Cnr Church Street
Tel: 773-3354

Antigua Beachcomber Hotel
Winthropes Bay
Tel: 462-3100. Fax: 462-4012
Email: beachcom@candw.ag

Antigua Village Condo Beach Resort
Dickenson Bay
Tel: 462-2930. Fax: 462-0375
Email: antiguavillage@candw.ag

ATS Car Rental & Limousine Service
Powell's
Tel: 562-1709. Fax: 461-5700
Email: ats@candw.ag

Blue Waters Hotel
Blue Waters
Tel: 462-0290
Fax: 462-0293
Email: bluewaters@candw.ag

B's Formal Wear
Market Street
Tel: 462-2314

Cocobay Resort
Valley Church
Tel: 562-2400
Fax: 562-2424
Email: cocobay@candw.ag

Coco Point Lodge
Codrington
Barbuda
Tel: 462-3816. Fax: 462-5340

Curtain Bluff Hotel
Old Road
Tel: 462-8400. Fax: 462-8409
Email: curtainbluff@candw.ag

E & G Bridal
Potter's Main Road
Tel: 462-4002. Fax: 462-5344

Eureka Events
Thames Street
Tel: 726-8400. Fax: 560-3654

Galleon Beach Club
English Harbour
Tel: 460-1024
Fax: 460-1450
Email: galleonbeach@candw.ag

Galley Bay Resort
Five Islands
Tel: 462-0302
Fax: 462-4551
Email: reservations@antigua-resorts.com

Hawksbill Beach Resort
Five Islands
Tel: 462-0301
Fax: 462-1515
Email: hawksbill@candw.ag

The Inn at English Harbour
English Harbour
Tel: 460-1014
Fax: 460-1603
Email: theinn@candw.ag

Janet's Bridal & Accessories
McKinnon's
Tel: 772-2580

Jolly Beach Resort
Bolans Village
Tel: 462-0061
Fax: 562-2302
Email: info@jollybeachresort.com

Jumby Bay Resort
Jumby Bay Island
Tel: 462-6000
Fax: 462-6020
Email: jumby@candw.ag

K Club
Barbuda
Tel: 460-0300
Fax: 460-0305
Email: kclubbarbuda@candw.ag

Long Bay Hotel
Long Bay
Tel: 463-2005
Fax: 463-2439
Email: longbay@candw.ag

Niobe's
Upper Church Street
St John's
Tel: 562-5767

Occasions Party Rentals
Lyons Estate
Tel: 463-8389
Fax: 460-8770

Rex Blue Heron
Johnsons Point
Tel: 462-8564
Fax: 462-8005

Rex Halcyon Cove
Dickenson Bay
Tel: 462-0256
Fax: 462-0271
Email: rexhalcyon@candw.ag

Sandals Antigua Resort & Spa
Dickenson Bay
Tel: 462-0267
Fax: 462-4135
Email: sandals@candw.ag

St James's Club
Mamora Bay
Tel: 460-0500
Fax: 460-3015
Email: reservations@antigua-resorts.com

Seabreeze Reception Hall
Seatons Main Road
Tel: 463-3401
Fax: 463-3401

Siboney Beach Club
Dickenson Bay
Tel: 462-0806
Fax: 462-3356
Email: siboney@candw.ag

Susie's Hotsauce
Upper North Street
Tel: 461-3065

Unas Bridal
Sutherlands
Tel: 462-4847

WINE & BEER RETAILERS (SEE LIQUOR, BEER & WINE RETAILERS)

YACHT RENTAL & CHARTER

Nicholsons Yachts Worldwide
English Harbour
Tel: 460-1530
Fax: 460-1531

Sunsail
Nelson's Dockyard
Tel: 463-6224
Fax: 460-2616
Email: charterservices@candw.ag

YACHT SALES & SERVICES

Antigua Slipway
English Harbour
Tel: 460-10556
Fax: 460-1566

Caribbean Connections
Antigua Yacht Club Marina
Tel: 460-2825
Fax: 460-2826

Hinkley Antigua Yacht Service
English Harbour
Tel: 460-2711
Fax: 460-3740

Nicholson Caribbean Yacht Sales
Falmouth
Tel: 460-1093
Fax: 460-1524

YACHT SUPPLIES & REPAIR

Antigua Rigging Ltd
Falmouth Harbour
Tel: 562-2651
Fax: 463-8575

Chippy / Seaward Sales
Cobbs Cross
Tel: 460-1832. Fax: 460-1491